ANTHROPOLOGICAL PAPERS
MUSEUM OF ANTHROPOLOGY, THE UNIVERSITY OF MICHIGAN
NO. 18

ARCHAEOLOGICAL INVESTIGATIONS
ON AGATTU, ALEUTIAN ISLANDS

by
ALBERT C. SPAULDING

ANN ARBOR
THE UNIVERSITY OF MICHIGAN, 1962

ISBN 978-1-949098-27-3 (paper)
ISBN 978-1-951519-49-0 (ebook)

CONTENTS

Introduction 3
    The Natural Environment 4
    Surface Features 6

Excavation Units 8
    Excavation Unit 1 9
    Excavation Unit 2 10
    Excavation Unit 3 10
    Excavation Unit 4 11
    Summary 16

Artifacts, Fauna, and Flora 17
    Chipped-stone Artifacts 18
    Pecked- and Ground-stone Artifacts 30
    Bone and Teeth Artifacts 33
    Other Materials 41
    Faunal Remains 41

Conclusion 42

References Cited 46

Plates 48

Tables

I. Artifact Counts by Provenience Unit—Excavation Unit 4 13
II. Distribution of Artifacts by Excavation Units Adjusted for Volume 17
III. Retouched Flakes and Blades by Excavation Units 19
IV. Flake-tool Proportions by Stratigraphic Positions— Excavation Unit 4 21
V. Proportions of Transverse Scrapers to All Classified Flake Tools 23
VI. Provenience of Lateral Scrapers 24
VII. Proportions of Bifacial Knives to All Chipped-stone Artifacts 26

INVESTIGATIONS ON AGATTU

Plates

I.	Fig. 1. Upper site. Fig. 2. Excavation Unit 1 completed	49
II.	Fig. 1. Site area, looking east. Fig. 2. Edge of site and Excavation Unit 4 refuse mound	50
III.	Fig. 1. Feature 1, Excavation Unit 4, partly cleared	51
	Fig. 2. Feature 4, Excavation Unit 4, looking northeast	51
IV.	Fig. 1. Feature 1, Excavation Unit 4, looking southwest	52
	Fig. 2. South wall, Excavation Unit 4	52
V.	Excavation Unit 4. Middle and west sections of south wall	53
VI.	Projectile points, blades, and drills	54
VII.	Bifacial blades	55
VIII.	Knife, scrapers, adze, and serrated flake	56
IX.	Projectile point	57
X.	Projectile points and drill	58
XI.	Projectile points	59
XII.	Projectile points	60
XIII.	Projectile points	61
XIV.	Transverse side scrapers	62
XV.	Blades; lateral and transverse side scrapers	63
XVI.	Blades	64
XVII.	Blades	65
XVIII.	Scrapers; chisels and adzes (?); ground-stone knife or point	66
XIX.	Scrapers, gravers, and serrated flake	67
XX.	Transverse and lateral side scrapers	68
XXI.	Blades and retouched flake knife or scraper	69
XXII.	Stone lamps or vessels	70
XXIII.	Barbed bone points and tooth ornaments	71
XXIV.	Bone and wood projectile points	72
XXV.	Bone flakers; bone and ivory wedges; bone handles (?)	73
XXVI.	Bone cylinders and prongs, or foreshafts, with beveled tongs	74
XXVII.	Bone prongs, or foreshafts, with beveled or subconical tongs	75
XXVIII.	Worked ribs	76
XXIX.	Baculum flakers; perforated bird bone; bone and fossil coral drill heads	77
XXX.	Bird-bone tools	78
XXXI.	Worked whalebone and bone picks	79

INTRODUCTION

The excavations on the island of Agattu described in this report were a part of a series of investigations in botany and anthropology conducted by The University of Michigan in the Aleutians in the period 1948-1951 with the aid of a grant from the Office of Naval Research. The Agattu party, Albert C. Spaulding, Wesley R. Hurt, and H. Alfred Miller, excavated at Krugloi Point, the northeastern tip of Agattu, from July 18 to August 24, 1949. Miller devoted some time to botanical field work in addition to assisting with the digging.

Our work was primarily the result of the enterprise and leadership of the late Professor H. H. Bartlett of the Department of Botany, who was in general charge of the Aleutian work. The assistance and advice of T. P. Bank, the ethnobotanist and field representative of the Michigan group, was invaluable to us. This assistance went well beyond the call of duty, and the hospitality of Mrs. Bank and Janet Fowler Bank was a most pleasant feature of our work. The help given to us by the military services was indispensable. It included transportation from and to Seattle and within the Aleutians, living quarters at the Naval Operating Base at Adak, loans of equipment for our stay at Agattu, and various other kinds of assistance. The greatest part of the burden we imposed fell on the Navy, but very substantial aid was given by the Army, the Air Force, and the Coast Guard.

The names of the personnel of the University Museums who gave technical advice on biological and other matters are listed in the appropriate sections of the report. Study of the human skeletal material has been undertaken by Professor William S. Laughlin of the University of Wisconsin; the result will be incorporated in his own publications on the physical anthropology of the Aleutians. For general advice and assistance, I am greatly indebted to Professor James B. Griffin, Director of the Museum of Anthropology at The University of Michigan.

I wish to single out for special recognition the work of Mrs. Anta Montet White. Her typological studies of the chipped-stone and bone artifacts form the basis for the discussion in the text, and the drawings shown as Plates VI, VII, and VIII are her work.

4   ARCHAEOLOGICAL INVESTIGATIONS ON AGATTU

NATURAL ENVIRONMENT AND SURFACE FEATURES

The Natural Environment

Agattu Island is the southernmost of the Near Islands, the most westerly of the Aleutian island groups. The other islands of the group are Attu, about 28 statute miles to the north-northwest, and the Semichi Islands (Alaid, Nizki, and Shemya), about 21 miles to the north-northeast. All of these islands are visible from Agattu on a clear day. The Near Islands are the most isolated in the entire archipelago. Kiska, the westernmost of the Rat Islands, lies 145 miles to the east with the small Buldir Island roughly half way between the two groups. To the west, the Commander Islands are the nearest land. They are 250 miles distant from Attu and about 138 miles off the coast of Kamchatka. Travel, even within the Near Islands, demands good boats and capable boatmen, and the two 70-mile passages of cold and stormy open water necessary to reach Kiska are downright formidable. The 250 miles to the Commanders and the 400 miles to Siberia would seem to be completely impracticable as routes for international and regular ventures in small open boats. On the basis of these facts and the knowledge that the Aleuts were capable boatmen one would expect a considerable amount of cultural interchange within the Near Islands, a persistent but not intensive connection with Kiska, and either no connection or very rare adventitious contacts with Siberia.

Agattu is shaped approximately like an isosceles triangle with a 10-mile-long base running in a north-south direction and the sides converging to a point about 14 miles west of the center of the base. The northern (Bering Sea) side is slightly longer than the southern; the airline distance from the northeastern tip of the island, Krugloi Point, to the west tip, Gillon Point, is about 18 miles, and a similar measurement from Gillon Point to Cape Sabok, the southeastern tip, is 15 miles. The coastline is not greatly indented, its total length probably not exceeding 60 miles. Proper harbors in the sense of deep, protected bays are lacking, although there are a number of comparatively shallow bays and coves. Most of the shoreline consists of cliffs, but short stretches of sand and cobblestone beaches occur with some frequency, especially where streams enter the ocean. Since the interior of the Island offered comparatively little in the way of resources to the Aleuts, it is not of great interest here. It is sufficient to note that it is a tundra-covered plateau for the most part reaching virtually to the shore. There is a small mountain range along the east half of the north shore. Frequent rocky points or cliffs extending to the water

NATURAL ENVIRONMENT AND SURFACE FEATURES   5

discourage hiking for any great distance along the beach, and the steep climb to the plateau and the soggy condition of the tundra at low altitudes make inland walking equally unpleasant. It is easy to understand why the Aleuts were such thoroughgoing boatmen.

The climate and biological resources of the Island are, so far as I could observe, typically Aleutian, and the excellent generalized description of Collins, Clark, and Walker (1945) is largely applicable. The weather is predominantly cool, windy, and wet, and rough seas and fog are common. On Agattu, as elsewhere in the Aleutians, the most striking botanical characteristic is the total absence of trees. This deficiency is, in part, made up by driftwood, but I do not know how plentiful the supply was in aboriginal times. In 1949, tons of wood were lodged on the beach in the vicinity of Krugloi Point, but it was almost entirely war debris from Attu and the Semichi Islands. The vegetation of beach, tundra, and village sites fits Walker's description well (Collins, Clark, and Walker, 1945, pp. 68-69). Various food plants, especially cow parsnips ("pootschky"), Eskimo potato (*Fritillaria camschatcensis*), and lupine are present. Strand wild rye grass, used for basketry, and kelp, from which fishing lines were made, are abundant. Of particular interest is the presence of monkshood (*Aconitum maximum*), the source of poison for whaling farther east in the archipelago. The animals of Agattu, like the plants, do not seem to differ in any important respect from the usual condition in the Aleutians. Arctic (blue) foxes are plentiful at present but are said to have been placed on the island recently (Collins, Clark, and Walker, 1945, p. 49). Sea mammals are abundant, especially sea lions and harbor seals. Sea otters were formerly common, and various of the smaller whales, dolphins, and porpoises are seen frequently. An extraordinary variety and number of sea birds are present, and fish are equally abundant. Among the latter are cod, halibut, salmon, Atka mackerel, herring, and other fish of economic importance. Marine invertebrates are also plentiful and were used extensively for food, to judge by the contents of the refuse deposits and the ethnographic literature. Sea urchins were the most important by refuse volume, but various mollusks were also found in some quantity. We did not see any octopus, a food and bait animal in the eastern part of the archipelago, but Clark states that they are common everywhere in the islands (Collins, Clark, and Walker, 1945, p. 59).

In summary, Agattu does not seem to have any special or unusual features of cultural importance arising from its situation or biotic characteristics. It is, in these respects, an Aleutian island much like other Aleutian islands, perhaps more isolated than most but certainly not impossibly so. It is said that Agattu supported thirty-one villages in the 1940's (Collins, Clark, and Walker, 1945, p. 20).

There remains, however, one feature of the natural environment which imposed its stamp on the prehistoric culture. This feature is the geological character of the island. Sharp observed (1946, pp. 193-94) that Agattu is largely composed of well-bedded sedimentary rocks and that these rocks are chiefly finegrained and rich in amorphous silica. There are some intrusions of porphyry, diabase, and trap. Perhaps 25 per cent of the section seen by Sharp consisted of impure chert. In the finegrained sedimentary rocks, strata from 1-to-3-inches thick predominate, and laminations and fracture systems are prominent. From the standpoint of the stone-flaker, abundant chippable stone is available in rock exposures along the beach, and it can be detached as flat plates. As a result, the art of striking long blades from a core is superfluous.

Surface Features

The sites reported here are situated roughly one-third of a mile west-northwest of Krugloi Point proper. As scaled from the 1952 Attu, Alaska, sheet of the United States Geological Survey Alaska Reconnaissance Topographic Series, Third Judicial Division, the geodetic co-ordinates are 52° 46' 00" of east longitude. The habitation areas here, as elsewhere in the Aleutians, are clearly defined by a prolific growth of broad-leaved dark vegetation, and it was apparent on first inspection that there are two village sites in the area. The first and easternmost site (Plate II) lies on low and gently sloping ground immediately above the storm beach and extends inland for an estimated maximum of 300 feet. Its beach frontage is on the order of 500 or 600 feet. The landward margin of the site is exceedingly irregular, and the total habitation area probably does not exceed 1.5 or 2 acres. Some 50 yards inland from the landward edge of the site a steep slope rises to the level of the interior plateau. By no means all of the low and relatively flat area in the vicinity is occupied by the site; lack of suitable ground was not a factor limiting the size of the village. The second site (Plate I) lies on higher and more steeply sloping ground several hundred yards to the west of the first. Separating the two is a nearly vertical rock escarpment about 20 feet high which trends at approximately a right angle to the generally east-west beach line. The western village begins close to the escarpment and extends westward for 200 to 300 feet. Although objective measurements are not available, it looks smaller than the lower

NATURAL ENVIRONMENT AND SURFACE FEATURES

village. It is also bounded by a cliff on the seaward (north) side, beneath which is a sheltered beach. Although these cliffs are steep, they can be climbed at a number of points, but the daily climbing between beach and village must have been inconvenient for the Aleuts. On the landward side, the steep slope to the interior plateau rises from the margin of the village site.

Cultural features are plainly visible on both sites. On the lower site, the general impression is one of a confused jumble of mounds and depressions. No well-defined house pits were seen. Maximum relief (from the top of the larger mounds to the bottom of an adjacent depression) was on the order of 5 feet. We inferred that the site had been inhabited for a comparatively long period in order to produce such a quantity of refuse and to so obliterate the house sites; but this reasoning does not explain why the house sites of the period of abandonment are not better marked. Presumably some of the depressions are house pits rather than more-or-less fortuitous intervals between refuse mounds. Perhaps the absence of clear outlines represents the combined result of house collapse with deposition of roof material and some filling in from adjacent refuse deposits. In any case, the absence of long rectangular pits is a sharp contrast to the situation in the upper village.

On the upper village, individual house pits are distinguishable. In particular, there is one plainly outlined example of the long rectangular pit of a communal house like that described in the early literature (Hrdlicka, 1945, p. 43 ff.). Regrettably, we failed to obtain measurements on this pit, but I would estimate that it is some 40 or 50 feet by 25 feet. The long axis is approximately at right angles to the beach. The edges of the pit are clearly defined by banks of earth. Other house depressions in the upper village are both smaller and less definite in shape; although some can be described as subrectangular. Excavation Unit 1 was placed in one of these subrectangular pits. The pit measures 25 feet on the long axis (from top to top of the end banks) and 19 feet on the transverse axis. Its long axis is roughly north-south and at right angles to the contour lines of the slope so that the south end is about 3 feet higher than the north end. The pit in the center is about 2.5 feet deep as measured from the top of the end walls.

There is no obvious basis for determining the relative age of the two sites on the evidence of surface characteristics. The comparatively steep slope and cliff boundaries make the upper site a decidedly inconvenient one from my point of view, but this was not necessarily the view of the Aleuts. One might be tempted to reason that the upper village was settled as an overflow from the larger lower village, the only flaw being that there is unoccupied ground available at the putatively more desirable site. The upper village is in a strong defensive situation, which may well be the reason for its existence. If this is the case, it could have served as a refuge for the people of the lower village, or it could have been built as a replacement of the lower village at some period of active warfare. However all this may be, the upper site looks younger. The contrast between its fairly well-defined house pits and less prominent refuse heaps and the chaotic topography of swells and hollows at the lower site suggests both that the latter has been abandoned for a longer time and that it was occupied for a longer period.

EXCAVATION UNITS

Our digging at Krugloi Point was divided into four excavation units, one (Excavation Unit 1) in the upper village, the other three in the lower village. All of the units were in the nature of exploratory cuts. Excavation Unit 1 was placed in a subrectangular depression in the east-central part of the upper village. It was intended to be a check on the amount of refuse to be expected in a house depression as well as a search for floor features. Excavation Unit 2 was a trench across a refuse mound near the beach at the extreme western part of the lower village. Excavation Unit 3 was a radial cut into a depression about 30 feet southeast of Excavation Unit 2. Here we hoped to uncover structural features of a house. Units 1, 2, and 3 were dug concurrently by the three members of the party, and the results obtained led us to decide that our remaining time would best be spent in a concentrated effort on a deep cut in a large refuse mound. Briefly, although Unit 1 was most productive of artifacts, no floor features were seen and the refuse was so deep that an expansion of the excavation to clear the house would have taken the rest of the field season. It seemed unwise to devote so much effort to obtaining perhaps some structural features and a collection of artifacts possibly representing a comparatively restricted period (or periods) of time. Unit 3 also failed to disclose any well-defined structural features and produced very few artifacts. Unit 2, the cut across a mound, showed a maximum depth of refuse of about 5 feet and nearly level strata, an encouraging situation for unraveling changes over time without too many technical complications, so we undertook to excavate the biggest trench we could manage in the biggest refuse mound in the lower village. The result was Excavation Unit 4, a 5-by-45-foot trench through a large mound in the south central part of the site about 100 yards southeast of Unit 2.

EXCAVATION UNITS 9

Our method of digging throughout was simply shovel and trowel, mostly shovel. Undoubtedly some artifacts were thrown away, but it is hoped that this unintentional discarding does not introduce any serious bias in the quantitative analysis of the various classes of artifacts recognized. We examined the dirt piles occasionally to check on the completeness of our collecting and failed to find any great amount of worked materials. Probably the greatest danger of underrepresentation is in the category of retouched or used flakes. Flakes were abundant, especially in Excavation Unit 4, and often a close look is required to distinguish between an unworked and a retouched specimen.

Excavation Unit 1 (Plate I, Figs. 1 and 2)

As I mentioned above, Excavation Unit 1 was a test pit in the upper village in a subrectangular depression thought to have been a house pit. The excavation was placed in the approximate center of the depression. When finished, it was a T-shaped pit averaging about 3.5 feet deep with a surface of 35 square feet and a volume (allowing for sidewall batter) of approximately 110 cubic feet. Although no internal house features were seen, the exposed vertical sections showed clearly that a house pit had been dug in older refuse and that the pit itself had then accumulated some fill after the abandonment of the house. Material from lower and upper refuse was segregated as soon as the nature of the situation was realized. The south to north (uphill-downhill) section showed the older refuse to be complexly lensed with the lenses parallel to the slope of the hill. This refuse was truncated by the house excavation, which in turn was partly filled by more nearly level deposits. Both lower and upper deposits showed a complicated succession of dark humus-like layers and lighter lenses composed in large part of crushed sea urchin shells. The deposits did not exhibit any pronounced steps or other evidence of constructional features. At the center of the house depression, the refuse was slightly more than 3 feet deep; here the older deposit was 1.2 feet thick and the overlying refuse measured about 2.1 feet. The upper refuse thinned rapidly toward the edges of the depression.

In terms of artifact productivity, both the upper and lower sections of Excavation Unit 1 were good. A total of 90 artifacts was recovered from the unit, 36 from the upper level and 54 from the lower deposits, a mean of about 0.8 artifacts per cubic foot. There was no significant difference between upper and lower deposits in the artifact to volume ratio if my estimate of 40 cubic feet for the upper and 70 cubic feet for the lower deposits is reasonably accurate. No special association of artifacts was seen, nor were there any burials or other features.

Excavation Unit 2

Excavation Unit 2 was a 3-by-10-foot trench cut through a small refuse mound a few feet from the storm beach at the west end of the lower site. Since our purpose here was simply to gain preparatory knowledge of the character of refuse heaps at the site, the specimens found were not kept by level. To our surprise, the refuse proved to be about 5 feet deep under the highest part of the mound. The vertical profile showed a substratum of sand and beach cobbles overlain by a complicated series of horizontal or gently sloping lenses of refuse which were in turn capped by a nearly featureless layer of black soil almost a foot thick. The absence of prominent black strata within the refuse and the numerous lenses suggest that the mound grew by substantially continuous deposition of small loads of refuse from nearby houses. The black topsoil is taken to represent a normal development of humus since deposition ceased. Fragments of sea urchin shells were the most noticeable component of the refuse; other prominent elements were fishbone and gastropod shells. Black dirt formed a considerable part of the content of most of the deposit and occasional, nearly pure, lenses were seen, but it seems to have been included as a part of the refuse rather than developed in place as humus on a stable surface. Bivalve shells, flakes of greenstone, fragments of mammal bone (whale and presumably seal or sea lion for the most part), bird bone, and artifacts were found throughout the deposit. The fishbone tended strongly to occur in compressed layers, and it is tempting to interpret each layer as a seasonal deposit. However, such an interpretation can be justified only by an intimate knowledge of the local natural history, which I do not possess. There were some 15 such layers superposed in the deepest part of the refuse. The estimated volume of the unit is about 130 cubic feet, and 36 artifacts were found, giving a figure of 0.3 artifacts per cubic foot, a result considerably lower than the 0.8 artifacts per cubic foot reported for Excavation Unit 1.

Excavation Unit 3

Excavation Unit 3 was a 4-by-8-foot trench extending from the edge to the center of a roughly circular depression thought to represent a house site. It was 30 feet southeast of Excavation Unit 1. The radial vertical section failed to show any clear structural features, the putative house wall consisting of no more than a humus-capped ridge of refuse like that seen in Excavation Units 1 and 2. The central part of the depression was filled with nearly 2 feet of featureless black humus. The section did indicate, however, that an excavation had been made in the beach cobble and sand stratum which underlay the humus and refuse. A weak shoulder was seen about 3 feet from the depression center, where the humus-substratum contact rose about 0.5 feet vertically in a horizontal distance of 1.5 feet. A few scraps of bones lay in the contact zone on the slope of the shoulder. Seven artifacts were found in Excavation Unit 3.

Excavation Unit 4 (Plate II, Fig. 2; Plate III, Figs. 1 and 2; Plate IV, Figs. 1 and 2; Plate V)

Excavation Unit 4 was a 5-by-45-foot trench situated about 300 feet to the southeast of Excavation Units 2 and 3. The trench was an east-west cut through what seemed to be the largest refuse mound in the lower village. The mound was near the inland margin of the site, perhaps 200 feet from the beach. Plate V illustrates the character of the refuse and the surface configuration of a part of the mound. Digging was conducted in one-foot levels as measured from the surface, and horizontal provenience was recorded by dividing the excavation into three 5-by-15-foot units designated the east, middle, and west sections. Four features, all burials, were recognized as special provenience units, and artifacts were associated with Features 1 and 3.

The nature of the deposits found in Excavation Unit 4 is summarized in Plate V, which represents the vertical section seen in the south wall of the trench for the entire middle section and 12 feet of the west section (Plate IV, Fig. 2 is a photograph of this section). The east section (not illustrated) was not excavated to the undisturbed substratum owing to lack of time; the 3-to-4-foot cut was only partly finished. An additional complication in the east section was the presence of Feature 1, a large burial pit which effectively obfuscated stratigraphic segregation to a depth of about 3 feet in the western third of the section. The undisturbed deposits of the east section, however, were quite similar to those illustrated. An important feature of the vertical section is the fact that the deposits are largely composed of irregular but essentially continuous and level deposits, especially below about 3.5 feet. The mound configuration seems to be the result of depositing a 3-foot-thick lens of additional refuse on a nearly flat surface or, alternatively, of producing the elevated central section by removing some of the deposits of the west section in digging a house pit. Since our arbitrary 1-foot cuts followed the surface configuration, it would appear that the vertical provenience units of the middle section reflect relative time of deposition fairly well, the major source of uncertainty being the irregular thicknesses of the strata. In the west section, however, our cuts represent relative age in only a very gross way. The cuts slant downward to the west, following the surface, and the "levels" cut diagonally across the deposits. The surface in the east section did not dip so sharply, and the situation was here more nearly comparable to the middle section.

The composition of the refuse is described in an impressionistic fashion in the legend of Plate V. The labels attached to the various strata are, of course, no more than characterizations of the more noticeable elements in each. In particular, artifacts, numerous greenstone flakes, larger slabs of rock, whale vertebrae, and fragments of whale and other mammal, bird, and fish bones were found in every level. In some cases both whalebones and rocks appeared to be burned, and in the middle section in the 3-to-4-foot level several small whale vertebrae were found in a group. At a depth of 6 feet, very close to the west end of the trench, we found a large fragment of whalebone in a vertical position surrounded by rocks. My field notes state that large fragments of rock were more common in the lower levels. Fragments of the skull of a human infant were found in the east section outside the area of Feature 1. The general appearance of the deposits suggests a two-part depositional history. The first is represented by the relatively level strata comprising, roughly, the lower two-thirds of the entire deposit. Here the presence of three thick strata with a substantial component of dark earth may indicate trampled refuse deposited on living levels at a comparatively slow rate. In contrast, the upper part looks like a rapid accumulation. The irregular lenses of more homogeneous debris can be interpreted as individual loads of trash dumped on the surface of an area used solely for refuse disposal. The mucky bottom of the deposit graded into a zone of dark, claylike material about 0.1-to-0.2-feet thick which in turn gave way to an undisturbed light brown clay with many fragments of greenstone. Some fragments of wood, including worked specimens, were found in this transition to the undisturbed substratum.

Several of the unworked pieces of wood were combined as carbon specimen M12 by the Michigan Memorial-Phoenix Project Radiocarbon Laboratory: two counts by the carbon black method yielded dates of 2500 ± 300 and 2630 ± 300 years ago (Crane, 1956,

p. 670). Accordingly, the best estimate for the beginning of deposition in the Excavation Unit 4 area is about 615 B. C. minus an unknown number of years to allow for the period elapsing between the death of the tree and its ultimate deposition in the refuse. Since the wood almost certainly drifted to Agattu from Siberia and may have lain on the beach for some time before it was used, this correction factor might be substantial. A second radiocarbon date was obtained from charcoal found in the 2-to-3-foot level in the east section of the unit. This specimen (M-13) was dated by the carbon dioxide method at 1300 ± 150 years ago, thus giving an estimate of about 1300 years for the accumulation of most of the mound.

A total of 675 artifacts was collected in Excavation Unit 4, of which 223 were found in the east section (including Feature 1), 235 in the middle section, and 217 in the west section. The estimated volume of material handled in the three sections was 240 cubic feet for the east section and 510 cubic feet each for the middle and west sections. Artifact productivity per cubic foot varied substantially: the number for the east section is 0.9 artifacts, for the middle section 0.5, and for the west section 0.4. The high ratio for the east section can be explained in part by the worked teeth in Feature 1 and perhaps by more careful excavating in the feature, but there seems to be a real difference after allowing for these factors. Table I indicates a similar variation among levels and further

TABLE I

ARTIFACT COUNTS BY PROVENIENCE UNIT
EXCAVATION UNIT 4

Level	Section		Section	
	East	Feature 1	Middle	West
0-1	15	50	58	11
1-2	54	..	39	45
2-3	83	..	34	52
3-4	21	..	13	40
4-5	..	..	17	18
5-6	..	..	22	14
6-7	..	..	20	4
7	..	..	32	33
Total	173	50	235	217

emphasizes the high productivity of the east section, where the volume per level for the upper 2 feet is reduced by Feature 1. It would appear, in general, that the upper 3 feet of debris is most productive, but the productivity does not seem closely associated with any particular lens or type of refuse. Our provenience discrimination, however, was not fine enough to permit any very meaningful judgments on this topic.

Feature 1 (Plate III, Fig. 1; Plate IV, Fig. 1).—Feature 1 was an approximately circular basinshaped pit about 6 feet in diameter and 2 feet deep containing a number of more-or-less disturbed skeletons. The center of the pit was nearly opposite the boundary between the middle and east sections of the unit, and its top was virtually at the surface of the mound. Aside from the skeletons, most of the pit fill consisted of sea urchin plates and spines, fishbone, mollusk shells, and other material characteristic of the refuse. Greenstone chips were unusually plentiful near the bottom of the pit; in fact, they formed a concentrated layer in some places. After the last burials were placed in the pit, seven slabs of rock, three whale vertebrae, and a large plate of whalebone were laid on, or among, the bodies. The skeletons seem to be the result of placing (or cramming) bodies into the pit. The presence of incomplete and greatly disordered skeletons suggests that the burials were made over a considerable time with later interments disturbing the bones already present. Our field notes indicated eight individuals the bones of which were unexplained. A census in the laboratory by Howard R. Sargent yielded a total of probably 11 individuals, distributed by age and sex as follows: 0-6 months and "infant," 2; 3-6 years, 1; 5-7 years, 1; "child," 1; 8-15 years, female?, 1; 15-21 years, sex unknown, 1; 18-25 years, female, 1; 20-26 years, female, 1; "adult," sex unknown, 1; and more than 50 years, male, 1.

The actual positions of the more-or-less intact skeletons suggest anything but a respectful placement of bodies in a ritually orthodox manner. Burials 1 and 2, both small children, were placed on the back with arms and legs flexed. Burial 3, the male of "more than 50 years," lay face and stomach down with arms and legs tightly drawn up. Burial 4, a woman of 20-26 years, lay on the left side with flexed arms and legs. Burial 5, an infant of less than 6 months, consisted chiefly of a skull, although there was some indication of flexed limbs. Burial 6, a girl of 8 to 15 years, was tightly flexed on the back and right side. Burial 7 consisted of a headless and otherwise incomplete adult resting on the stomach. Bones of at least 3 individuals were labeled in the field as "Burial 7," but most of them pertain to the headless adult; the other two individuals were represented by assorted fragments of an infant and an individual from 15-21 years of age. Burial 8, a woman of 18-25 years, lay in a contorted position on the back and right side with the spine bent backward and twisted, the head bent far backward, and the arms and legs tightly flexed. In addition to these numbered burials, other bones were noted in the field but could not be described in terms of body placement. For example, a few articulated vertebrae, a tibia, and a few foot bones were found together between Burials 6 and 8 at the bottom of the pit. The orientation of the skeletons appeared to be quite random. There seemed to be something on the order of three main stages in the accumulation of the burials. Burials 3, 6, and 8 were placed on the bottom of the pit and perhaps had disturbed a still earlier burial (Plate IV, Fig. 1). Burials 4 and 7 overlie these lower burials and are overlain by the remaining burials—all children or infants. The rock and whalebone at the top of the fill completed the deposit. The feature, as a whole, is definitely a unit—a pit filled with bodies—although the filling covered a long enough period of time so that the later interments disturbed the earlier ones. I would suppose that the whole process took place within a few years. Since Feature 1 intrudes the uppermost layers of the mound, it clearly postdates the cessation of refuse deposition in this area.

The only grave goods surely associated with Feature 1 were 12 grooved or perforated teeth of sea mammals (probably all sea lion) found on or near Burial 4 (Plate XXIII F, G). An imitation grooved tooth of bone (Plate XXIII D) and a perforated tooth (Plate XXIII K) were found in the pit fill but were not associated with any burial. In addition to these worked teeth, 4 others were found in the upper foot of the middle section and may well be a part of the grave goods. The teeth were scattered more-or-less randomly, and we were unable to determine from their position whether they represented a necklace or some other type of ornament. One grooved tooth (Plate XXIII E) and 3 serrated greenstone blades were found near the skull of Burial 6, and a barbed bone fragment (Plate XXIII C), 8 worked bones, a grooved-stone line sinker, and other fragments of worked stone were found in the pit fill. Presumably most were simply included in the refuse used to fill the pit.

Feature 2.—Feature 2 was a partly excavated burial of an infant. The broken skull and mandible projected from the north wall 2.5 feet from the west end of Excavation Unit 4 at a depth of 5.0 feet below the surface. Vertebrae extended into the wall. The mandible was inverted, suggesting some disturbance. Refuse strata above the bones were unbroken.

Feature 3.—Feature 3 was also a burial projecting from the north wall of Excavation Unit 4. Its position was 10 feet east of the west end of the trench at a depth of 6.7 feet. The distal parts of the femora, the tibiae and fibulae, some foot bones, and a few hand bones were seen. The bones were in approximate order and suggest a supine extended burial. The bones are those of an adult, probably a male. Several rocks (including a lamp fragment) and a piece of whalebone lay between the legs; they were, perhaps, placed on the body at the time of its burial. We would observe no clear trace of a pit in the vertical wall over the bones. The body must have been either placed in a very shallow pit or simply laid on the then existing surface of the refuse.

Feature 4 (Plate III, Fig. 2).—Feature 4 was another supine, extended burial of an adult, this time quite clearly a male over 28 years of age. The body was oriented east-west with the head to the east. The left side of the skeleton protruded from the north wall in the west half of the middle section of Excavation Unit 4. The body had been laid on a sloping refuse surface so that the head was about 0.8 feet lower than the feet. There was no clear evidence of a pit fill above the burial; an extensive layer of predominantly dark earth about 1 foot thick covered the burial and a layer of sea urchin shell on which it rested. We judged that the grave could have been no more than a very shallow pit in this dark layer, which may have been a living level. The skull was about 7 feet below the surface, the foot bones about 6 feet, which indicated that the burial was made at a quite early stage in the accumulation of the mound. It was, however, at a slightly higher stratigraphic level than Feature 3. No artifacts or other objects were associated with the burial. The top of the cranium had been removed by cutting before burial.

SUMMARY

Artifact counts, volume of excavation, and other data for all excavation units are indicated in Table II, below. The fourth column, "Expected Artifacts," is simply the number of artifacts which would be expected if each of the excavation units had the same number of artifacts per cubic foot as did Krugloi Point as a whole. Thus the entry for Excavation Unit 1 was computed as $110/1,555 \times 810 = 57.3$ artifacts. The fifth column, "Difference," was obtained by subtracting the expected number of artifacts from the number actually found. Units 1 and 4E have many more artifacts

TABLE II

DISTRIBUTION OF ARTIFACTS BY EXCAVATION
UNITS ADJUSTED FOR VOLUME

Excavation Unit	Volume (cubic feet)	Number of Artifacts	Expected Artifacts	Difference
1	110	90	57.3	+32.7
2	130	36	67.7	-31.7
3	55	7	28.6	-21.6
4E	240	224	125.0	+99.0
4M	510	235	265.7	-30.7
4W	510	218	265.7	-47.7
Total	1,555	810	810.0	....

than would be expected on this basis, and the remaining units have less. There is no obvious explanation for this notable difference in artifact productivity. One might be tempted to reason that living areas such as the house pit of Excavation Unit 1 would tend to have more artifacts than mere mounds of food debris, but the productive east section of Unit 4 was not more clearly a living area than the less productive middle and west sections. Moreover, although Unit 3 was thought to be a house pit, it contained few artifacts, and the upper, strongly lensed levels of the middle and west sections of Unit 4 contained more artifacts than did the possible living levels represented by the darker and more level lower strata. It seems unlikely that the sole explanation is variation in our collecting efficiency, and I can conclude only that, for some unknown reason, artifacts were not distributed evenly through the deposits.

ARTIFACTS, FAUNA, AND FLORA

A total of 819 artifacts was collected at Krugloi Point, of which 810 have specific excavation provenience, 8 are unassigned owing to faulty field work, and 1 is a surface find from the beach in front of the lower village. The distribution of artifacts as such has been discussed in the preceding section. Here I shall take up description and classification, functional inferences, and distribution by provenience units within and between classes. The major categories of organization are the familiar classes of material and, in the case of stone artifacts, techniques of manufacture. Classes of material are stone, bone and teeth, shell, and wood; within stone, chipped (including chipped and polished specimens) and pecked specimens are treated as if they were major categories. Mineralogical identification of stone artifacts was done by Glenn Kleinsasser with the aid of various members of the Department of Mineralogy at The University of Michigan. We are also indebted to William R. Farrand for assistance in identification. Worked bone and teeth were identified by comparison with specimens in the University Museums, and we are most grateful for the help given by William H. Burt and Emmet T. Hooper of the Museum of Zoology and by Claude W. Hibbard of the Museum of Paleontology.

Faunal specimens other than artifacts consist of unworked bird and mammal bones and teeth and various kinds of marine shells. Space limitations of the transport facilities available prevented us from making an extensive collection of unworked specimens, consequently, we can attempt no more than a list of animals present. In addition to the authorities noted above, Henry van der Schalie of the Museum of Zoology, The University of Michigan, identified the shellfish, and Robert N. Storer, Harrison B. Tordoof, and Norman L. Ford, also of the Museum of Zoology, identified the birds.

The floral specimens consist entirely of 10 fragments of wood found in the mucky deposit at the base of the refuse mound explored by Excavation Unit 4. We have not attempted specific identification of this wood.

Chipped-stone Artifacts (Plates VI-XXI)

Artifacts of chipped stone are the most common class from Krugloi Point; 384 specimens were collected, and numerous unworked flakes were present in refuse deposits. Already mentioned is the fact that Agattu has an abundant local source of raw material in the form of numerous exposures of stratified siliceous stone suitable for chipping. Most of the material from which the artifacts were made can be called greenstone, but minor amounts of chert (tan or gray in color) and perhaps slate are also present. Both stratification and jointing are characteristic of the Agattu deposits, and the raw material of the stone chipper was, for the most part, flat plates rather than nodules of stone. As a result, there are no examples of what could properly be called cores. All of the specimens are retouched flakes, bifaces, or, more rarely, simply tabular fragments with retouched edges. No specimen had a maximum thickness of more than about an inch, and most were considerably thinner. Both percussion and pressure flaking were employed. The latter is usually done skillfully, and, in the case of some projectile points, takes the form of delicate, oblique ripple flaking. A few specimens show both flaking and grinding.

Distribution of chipped-stone artifacts.—The broadest division of the chipped-stone artifact is represented by the 2 categories of unifacial and bifacial tools. We have used "retouched flakes" and "blades" as synonyms for the categories. A few specimens are assigned to one or the other of these classes with a certain amount of strain; 2 specimens are flaked on one side and ground on the other, and a few pieces are essential tabular fragments with retouched edges (Plate XXA, for example). If we ignore this difficulty, the classification yields 167 retouched flakes and 217 blades for the pooled specimens for all excavation units, or in relative terms, about 43 and 57 per cent respectively. Table III presents the counts for the 2 categories by excavation units (Feature 1 is included in Excavation Unit 4E, and 2 artifacts of unknown provenience are omitted):

TABLE III

RETOUCHED FLAKES AND BLADES BY
EXCAVATION UNITS

Artifact Class	Excavation Unit							
	1U	1L	2	3	4E	4M	4W	Total
Flakes	17	9	6	4	40	66	24	166
Blades	9	32	8	3	61	57	46	216
Total	26	41	14	7	101	123	70	382

Since the contrasting surface configurations of the upper and lower villages suggest an age difference, it seemed possible that the ratio of flake tools to blade tools might furnish evidence of a quantitative difference related to this suspected chronological distinction. As a first step in analyzing the ratios, a contingency chi-square for the entire distribution was computed to test whether any significant differences are present. The result is significant in the statistical sense; chi-square for 5 degrees of freedom (Excavation Units 2 and 3 were combined because of low totals) is 21.9, a value which would be equaled or exceeded less than once in a thousand trials through chance alone. It is reasonable to infer that the variations in the ratios of flake tool to blade tool exhibited by the seven excavation units cannot be explained by mere sampling vagaries--we cannot view the observed proportions as representing seven blindfolded dips into a large barrel of thoroughly mixed flake and blade tools. This being the case, it is worth while to examine the table more closely to identify the source of the large chi-square. An obvious device is to pool the counts for the two units of the upper village, Excavation Units 1U and 1L, and compare them with the combined counts of the five lower village units. The result is distressing from the standpoint of one looking for a neat distinction between the two sites: chi-square for 1 degree of freedom is no more than 0.6, a value which would be equaled or exceeded more than 30 per cent of time with nothing more than ordinary sampling fluctuations. Accordingly, the upper and lower sites taken as units must be considered virtually identical so far as the proportions of flake tools and blade tools are concerned. Further analysis shows that the source of the large over-all variation lies in fluctuations within the upper and the lower sites. Within the two units of the upper site, the percentage of flake tools is 65 for the upper level and 22 for the lower, a substantial and statistically significant difference. Within the lower village, the relatively large number of flake tools (54 per cent) from Unit 4M seems to be the chief source of heterogeneity. Under these circumstances, it can hardly be argued that there is a systematic relationship between planimetric position and the flake tool-blade tool ratio.

A final aspect of the problem is possible relationship to stratigraphic position. In the case of the two units from the upper village, relative age is known by superposition, and the proportion of flake tools in the lower level is about 22 per cent, in the upper level about 65 per cent. Moreover, these differences are statistically significant, that is, they cannot reasonably be attributed to the fluctuations expected of two random samples drawn from a single population. I have attempted to investigate the stratigraphically controlled specimens of Excavation Unit 4 in the same manner by pooling the upper 3 feet of the west and middle sections with the east section (where total depth was a little more than 3 feet) as an upper unit and similarly combining the lower levels of the middle and west sections as a lower unit. The result is set out in Table IV. Chi-square for this table is no more than 0.4 for 1 degree of freedom, indicating that the 4U and 4L proportions are identical for all practical purposes. There is no evidence of a shift in proportion over the time span represented by Excavation Unit 4. As a final observation, the proportions of flake tools within the three sections

TABLE IV

FLAKE-TOOL PROPORTIONS BY STRATIGRAPHIC POSITION
EXCAVATION UNIT 4

Provenience Unit	All Chipped Stone (Number)	Flake Tools (Number)	Flake Tools (Proportion)
4 Upper ..	259	116	0.448
4 Lower ..	35	14	0.400
Total ..	294	130	

of Excavation Unit 4, upper, are 4E, 39 per cent; 4M upper, 55 per cent; and 4 W upper, 35 per cent. These variations are statistically significant, reflecting the earlier observation of heterogeneity within the planimetric units of the lower village. The heterogeneity is not removed by controlling the vertical locus.

In summary, the flake tool to blade tool ratio does not exhibit any clear systematic relationship to either horizontal or vertical locus. Variations within strata and within horizontal loci seem to be the major source of the heterogeneity observed. No estimate of within stratum heterogeneity is available for the upper village, however, and it is possible to postulate an increase in the proportion of flake tools to blade tools over the time span represented by the excavated deposits there. Such an inference would be quite uncertain in my opinion in view of the generally capricious behavior of even arbitrarily segregated units in one refuse mound. In terms of human behavior, I would infer that the occupants of Krugloi Point did not discard chipped-stone tools randomly. There are areas of concentration of flake tools and of blade tools which misrepresent the actual proportions characteristic of any given period, and this situation prevents our limited excavations from revealing any systematic changes that may have taken place.

Retouched flakes.--The major attributes considered in classifying the flake tools consist of the position of the marginal retouching with respect to the bulb of percussion, whether the retouching was directed from one or both faces of the implement, and the general shape of the working edge. The combinations of attributes noted correspond for the most part to the quite familiar functional and formal categories of end scrapers, lateral and transverse side scrapers, convex-edged knives, and so on. There are also a number of fragmentary specimens of flake tools which cannot be assigned to the more detailed categories.

End scrapers (Plate VIII-I, Plate XIXD, Plate XVIIIC. This term is used in the conventional sense to imply a relatively narrow tool with a single-beveled scraping margin at the end. The retouch of the scraping edge is directed from the bulbar surface to the back of the flake, and the sides of the scraper are also retouched, presumably to give the desired shape. Only three examples of end scrapers were noted. The specimen of Plate VIII-I and XIXC has a convex scraping edge and an ovoid outline, but the remaining two have a rectangular working end. All of the end scrapers were found in Excavation Unit 4, their detailed proveniences being 4W, 1-2 feet; 4W, 4-5 feet; and 4M, below 6 feet.

Gravers (Plate VIII, G and H; Plate XIX, E and C). This term is used in the sense of Laughlin (Laughlin and Marsh 1956, p. 8) to indicate the intersection of 2 retouched margins to form a sharp or slightly rounded tip. It should be noted that our specimens, unlike Laughlin's Umnak examples, are not made on lamellar flakes. Only 3 examples, 2 of which are illustrated, were found at Krugloi Point. One (Plate VIIIH) has a shaping retouch on one margin directed from the back of the flake to the bulbar surface. Two gravers were found in Excavation Unit 4, Middle Section, one at 1-2 feet, the other at 4-5 feet. The remaining graver came from the upper level of Excavation Unit 1.

Transverse scrapers (Plates VIIIA, B, C, M; XIVA-E; XXB, D, E; XXI, D). Transverse scrapers are flakes with a working edge of the single-beveled scraper type on a long margin opposite to the bulb of percussion. Together with lateral scrapers, they make up the more general class of side scrapers. The illustrated specimens provide a good idea of the size and shape of the transverse scrapers. Working edges are usually convex or straight, and the retouching has produced either an even or a slightly denticulated scraping edge. The denticulated edge is a little more common. A few transverse scrapers (10 out of a total of 58) also have lateral retouching, probably to give the tool the desired shape. The specimen figured as Plate XXID, although formally a transverse scraper, is so different in shape from the ordinary examples as to indicate a special function. The carefully retouched edge is the concave side of the beak, and the top of the beak is somewhat worn, suggesting that the tool was an Aleut equivalent of a modern linoleum knife. Most of the transverse scrapers are large enough to be used without any handle, and the side opposite the scraping edge is usually thick owing to the presence of the bulb of percussion.

The provenience of the 58 transverse scrapers is: Excavation Unit 1, Upper, 6 specimens; Unit 1, Lower, 5; Unit 2, 1; Unit 3, 2;

Unit 4W, 0-3 feet, 7; Unit 4W, below 3 feet, 1; Unit 4M, 0-3 feet, 20; Unit 4M, below 3 feet, 2; and Unit 4E, 14.

TABLE V

PROPORTIONS OF TRANSVERSE SCRAPERS TO ALL CLASSIFIED FLAKE TOOLS

Excavation Unit	Classified Flake Tools	Transverse Scrapers	Proportion of Transverse Scraper
1U	11	6	0.545
1L	12	5	0.417
4U	77	41	0.532
4L	8	3	0.375
Total	108	55	....

Table V summarizes the proportions of transverse scrapers to all classified flake tools. The data are pooled so as to give a statistically workable analysis of changes in proportions by gross provenience units. The upper 3 feet of Unit 4 (4E and Feature 1, 4M 0-3 feet, and 4W 0-3) comprise 4U. Units 2 and 3 are omitted altogether. A contingency chi-square for 3 degrees of freedom is 0.6, indicating that there is no good evidence of a significant difference in proportions among the units considered. It must be admitted that such a computation is on the precarious side because of the small number of specimens in three of the units, especially in pooled Unit 4L, but a more conservative view would come to the same conclusion: the evidence does not suggest culturally meaningful differences among the provenience units in the ratio of transverse scraper to all flake tools. Accordingly, the best description is that the site as a whole shows a transverse scraper to all flake tool ratio of 58:117 or very close to 50:50.

Lateral scrapers (Plates VIIID, E, K; XVB, D-F; XVIIIG, H; XIXA, B, F). As was implied above, lateral scrapers are scrapers with a long single-beveled working edge prepared on one or both of the margins of the flake adjacent to the margin of the bulbar end. For the most part, lateral scrapers were made on blade-like flakes, that is, they tend to be relatively narrow. The retouched side (or sides) is often straight, but convex scraping edges are also present. In some cases the scraping edge is very little modified from the original configuration of the flake. Occasionally, wear flaking is present on the bulbar surface. The range of size and shape and the general character of the chipping is represented by the illustrations. Lateral scrapers tend to be less robust than transverse scrapers, and this difference, perhaps, has functional significance.

Twenty-two lateral scrapers were found, of which 14 have a single scraping edge and 8 a bilateral working edge retouch. Table VI, below, indicates their distribution by provenience units, pooling the upper 3 feet of Unit 4 Middle Section and 4 West Section 23 4WU and the below 3-feet deposits as 4ML and 4WL. The data of the table do not suggest any pronounced clustering of the lateral

TABLE VI

PROVENIENCE OF LATERAL SCRAPERS

Class	Excavation Unit									
	1U	1L	2	3	4E and Feat. 1	4MU	4ML	4WU	4WL	Total
Single Edge ...	..	1	..	..	3	7	..	3	..	14
Double Edge ...	..	..	..	..	1	3	1	3	..	8
Total ...	..	1	..	..	4	10	1	6	..	22

scrapers by provenience unit, and the total numbers are too low to detect any small but significant differences. Twenty of the 22 specimens come from the upper levels of Excavation Unit 4, but a comparison with the lower levels of the unit fails, owing to the small number of specimens. A suggestion of increasing frequency of lateral scrapers through the time of accumulation of the Excavation Unit 4 deposits is possible, but more data are needed before the hypothesis can be accepted or rejected at any reasonable level of probability.

Flake knives. Fourteen of the flake tools show bifacial edge retouching rather than the scraper style of retouching from the bulbar face only. In a few cases this bifacial retouching is confined to a small part of the working edge and is perhaps merely the result of use pressure, but more often there is a definite double-beveled margin of the kind usually considered a knife edge. Seven of the double-beveled tools are like the transverse scrapers. In every feature except the cutting edge they are robust, roughly triangular flakes with the knife edge on the base of the triangle and

ARTIFACTS, FAUNA, AND FLORA   25

opposite to the bulb of percussion. They would seem to be the
functional equivalent of the familiar Eskimos ulu. The saw-like
specimen illustrated as Plate VIIF and XIXG is a special case. It
has one serrated edge prepared by pressure flaking from both
sides.

All of the knife-edged flakes were found in Excavation Unit 4;
12 were in the upper 3 feet and 2 at a greater depth. The numbers
available are too small for significance testing, and the meaning of
the complete absence of flake knives from Excavation Units 1, 2,
and 3 is not clear.

Bifacial Blades

Nearly all of the identifiable bifacially flaked blades are either
more or less ovate knife-like artifacts of various sizes and degrees
of finish or quite neatly made projectile points. Minor categories
include one drill, seven chisel-ended blades, a chopper-like specimen, and a tool with one polished side which we judge to be a planing adze. The tally by major classes is: knife blades and incomplete specimens thought to be fragments of knife blades, 130; lance
and projectile points, 45; other classes, 10; and unclassified fragments, 32.

Knives (Plates VIIA-G, J, K?; VIIIL; XVA; XVIB-E; XVIIA-F;
XXIA, C, E). —Most of the complete knives are illustrated. As can
be seen, the range in size and shape is considerable, although we
are unable to detect any clear subclasses within the general category. The observed variations seem, in the main, attributable to
differences in the size and shape of the tabular blocks from which
the knives were made, to the stage of completion or amount of wear
on completed specimens, and to lack of rigidly defined standards on
the part of the makers. A few fragmentary specimens may be ex-
ceptions to the generalization; they show slight constrictions which
could mark the beginning of a tang (Plates VIIJ and XVIIB, for example). The specimens illustrated as Plates VIIK and IXD and
VII-I and IXE have tangs, but they may be large projectile points
rather than knives. If tanged knives are present at Krugloi Point
at all they are certainly rare, and the ovoid or modified ovoid
shape is characteristic. The dimensions of the complete specimens
vary considerably. A good example of a very large knife is the
specimen of Plates VIIB and XVIIE, which is 16.5 cm long, 5.7 cm
broad, and 1.8 cm in maximum thickness. Perhaps the smallest
knife is the specimen of Plates VIIIL and XVIIA; it is 8.3 by 2.5 by
0.5 cm in its major dimensions. Most of the fragments seem to be
on the larger end of the range. The primary flaking is character-

istically a neat percussion type, and usually one or both edges show some pressure flaking as well. This edge retouch ranges from a steep crude style, perhaps resulting from use, to a careful trimming comparable to that seen on projectile points. Several knives have one edge somewhat dulled, possibly by deliberate grinding, and the opposite edge sharply retouched. Others, however, have both edges dulled, and here the edge wear, probably, is simply the result of use. Several specimens are crudely flaked and thick in transverse section (Plate XVIIC, for example); these are probably unfinished knives or even choppers. Many knives exhibit flat areas that are remnants of bedding or jointing planes on the original block.

The distribution of knives and probable fragments of knives is: Unit 4E and Feature 1, 43 specimens; 4M 0-3 feet, 39; 4M below 3 feet, 6; 4W 0-3 feet, 24; 4W below 3 feet, 1; Units 2 and 3, 0; Unit 1 Upper Level, 3; and Unit 1 Lower Level, 14. Since knives and fragments constitute a large proportion of the bifacial tools, I have compared them with the total chipped-stone artifacts in Table VII in order to investigate differences in relative quantity

TABLE VII

PROPORTIONS OF BIFACIAL KNIVES TO ALL CHIPPED-STONE ARTIFACTS

Excavation Unit	Total Chipped Artifacts	Knives	Proportion of Knives
4U ...	259	106	0.409
4L ...	35	7	0.200
2 and 3 ...	21	...	...
1U ...	26	3	0.115
1L ...	41	14	0.341
Total ...	382	130	

among the provenience units. Table VII again groups Units 4E, Feature 1, and 4M and 4W 0-3 feet as an upper level of Unit 4 and all deposits below 3 feet as a lower unit. Units 2 and 3 are pooled because of their small total number of chipped-stone artifacts. The differences in proportions are statistically significant. Unit 4U has a high proportion (41 per cent) of knives and the earlier 4L a lower proportion (20 per cent), suggesting an increase in popularity over the period of the Unit 4 deposits. Moreover, the three planimetric

ARTIFACTS, FAUNA, AND FLORA 27

divisions of 4U are homogeneous, the percentages ranging from 39 (unit 4MU) to 43 for 4E plus Feature 1. Excavation Units 2, 3, and 1U have lower percentages, but the Unit 1L proportion is 34 per cent, the mean proportion for the site as a whole. If we view these variations as solely the product of change through time, then bifacially flaked knives increased in popularity from the 4L period to the 4U period and decreased from 1L to 1U. Excavation Units 2 and 3 would represent a period at the beginning or end of the sequence when knives of this kind were rare or entirely absent. An alternative view is to question the reliability of the observed proportions as a sample of the true proportions and to reject time inferences based on the samples. This interpretation is supported by the inconsistency of the subdivisions of Excavation Unit 4 in the matter of flake-tool proportions discussed earlier, but it is definitely not supported by the consistency of the three divisions of the upper levels of Unit 4 with respect to the knife to all chipped-tool ratio. The absence of bifacial knives in Units 2 and 3 is particularly puzzling, since no functionally suitable substitute occurred; it is difficult to believe that the people who made these deposits had no knives at all, and this situation again casts doubt on the representativeness of the sample. In summary, there is evidence on the basis of the proportion of bifacially flaked knives as a component of the total chipped-stone inventory and the unimodal curve concept of a time sequence of 4L, 4U, 1L, and 1U (or the reverse) with Units 2 and 3 falling at one or the other end of the sequence. The capricious behavior of the samples in other matters indicates caution, however, and probably the best verdict is "not proven."

Lance and projectile points (Plates VI, IX-XIII).—A total of 45 projectile points or fragments judged to be of projectile points were found. All of the complete specimens and many of the fragments are illustrated. The specimens illustrated on Plates VIC and XIIIG, VII-I and IXE, and VIIK and IXD are somewhat dubious members of the projectile point class, and a few of the fragments may be confused with knives on the one hand and with drills on the other. There are two reasonably clear types represented, a long, slender lance point and a smaller-shouldered dart point, as well as several other forms which may or may not represent consistent and functionally significant patterns.

Lance points are illustrated as Plates VIK and IXF, IXG, and the fragments of Plate IXC, XIID, and XIIIF may be from lances. Plates XIE and XIIE are probably inverted illustrations of the polish and grinding which they exhibit. These points are very much like the Attu specimen illustrated by Jochelson (1925, text fig. 33, p. 65) and described as used "both in attacking sea mammals when in their rookeries and men." As can be seen in the illustrations, the points are long and extraordinarily slender (the complete specimen is 14.9 cm long and 2.0 cm wide) and have markedly serrated edges. The basal end is elliptical in shape with ground edges; the ground portion extends upward for 2.5 cm on the specimen of Plate IXG. The transverse section is lozenge-shaped and quite thick, about 1.0 cm on both of the illustrated specimens. There is a definite central ridge on both faces. Some of the fragments thought to be from points of this type have thinner and more nearly lenticular transverse sections. The points are finished by pressure flaking which is rather coarse by comparison to the smaller types of points. Both of the illustrated specimens have groups of short transverse grooves or tick marks on their faces. On the specimen of Plate IXF they are confined to 1 face (that illustrated): beginning at 3.5 cms above the base, there are first a pair on the right margin, still another pair on the right margin only 1.5 cm below the tip, and, finally, a group of 4 across the face at the tip. The individual marks are about 3 to 5 mm long and the members of a set are about the same distance apart. The specimen of Plate IXG has 2 marks on one face, somewhat thinner and longer and running from the center to the right margin that divide the point approximately into thirds. The opposite face has 3 marks— 2 run from about the center to the right margin and the third is a short tick on the right margin a few millimeters above the base. The other 2 marks are situated 5.0 and 12.5 cms from the basal extremity. Similar scratches occur on 1 other lance point fragment and on some of the dart points. They are presumably property marks. Somewhat similar marks are found on parts of bone projectile heads (Jochelson, 1925, p. 93).

Nine specimens are definite, or probable, members of the lance class, of which 4 lack the basal grinding described for the illustrated specimens. The provenience of the lance points is: Unit 1, Lower Level, 1 specimen; Unit 2, 2 doubtful specimens; Unit 3, 1 specimen; Unit 4 West Section, 0-3 feet, 2 specimens; Unit 4 West Section, 3-4 feet, 1 specimen; Unit 4 Middle Section, 0-3 feet, 1 specimen; and Feature 1, 1 specimen. These counts are obviously too small for any detailed analyses. About all that can be said is that there is no clear evidence of any concentration.

Shouldered dart points and fragments probably representing this class are illustrated by Plates VIA, F, H, and I; XA, B, and D-H; XIA-D, F-H; XIIA, and XIIIA and C. The class is characterized by its rather small, slender blades, slight but definite shoulders, and rectangular tangs. To judge from size and general appearance, these specimens served as points for the darts used in

ARTIFACTS, FAUNA, AND FLORA

hunting the smaller sea mammals. Range in size and shape is illustrated adequately. Details of interest are the occasional presence of serrations just above the shoulder, the fine ripple flaking exhibited by most specimens, and the rare presence of grooves or ticks of the same sort as those described for the lances as property marks. One specimen (Plate VIH) has a tang ground on one side. The points are typically lozenge-shaped in transverse section. The frequency distribution of 19 reasonably clear examples of the class is: Excavation Unit 1U, 0 specimens; Unit 1L, 2 specimens; Unit 2, 4 specimens; Unit 4U, 9 specimens; and Unit 4L, 4 specimens. Again the tallies are too small for detailed analysis, and all I can suggest is that the class is well distributed over the excavation units.

The remainder of the supposed projectile points consist of fragments of blades or tangs which could belong to the lance or dart classes and a few distinctive specimens. The specimen of Plates VIB and XIIB is unusual for its short, wide shape and its terminal edge rather than point. The specimen of Plates VIC and XIIIG also has a rounded end and what appears to be a very short and broad tang below weak shoulders; it may be a knife rather than a projectile point. The knife or projectile point of Plates VII-I and IXE has been mentioned above. The pointed-tanged artifact of Plates VIJ and XIIIE is probably a projectile point and is the only example of this shape; it was retouched from opposite sides to give a parallelogram cross section. Plate IXA illustrates what may be the inverted base of a heavy lance, but no grinding is present, and the specimen may be a knife or projectile point with a broken tang. Plates VID and IXB figure a fragment of a neatly made implement having a slightly concave tip or base. The implement of Plate XIIF is a coarsely flaked leaf-shaped blade with a broken base.

Other bifacial tools.—We have enumerated several minor classes of tools. One specimen (Plate VIE) we judge to be a drill. It is neatly finished by pressure flaking, has a rather lozenge-shaped transverse section, and shows a slight amount of wear on the base. It was found in Excavation Unit IVW in the 1-to-2-foot level. The specimen illustrated as Plates VIIH and XVIIID is chisel-like in form. Both ends are straight and the transverse section approaches a plano-convex shape. The straighter side is somewhat worn, or ground, for its entire length, a circumstance not easily explained by the presumed chisel function. The specimen came from Unit IVE, 2-to-3-foot level. A total of 7 tools thought to be chisels were noted, but their proveniences do not seem to indicate any systematic distribution. The tally is: Unit 1, lower, 2 specimens; Unit 4, Feature 1, 2 specimens; Unit 4E, 0-1 feet, 1 specimen; Unit 4E, 2-3 feet, 1 specimen; Unit 4M, 1-2 feet, 1 specimen. The implement illustrated on Plates VIIIJ and XVIIIA is probably a small adze. Its lower side is quite well polished, and the upper side is also polished, although not to such an extent as to obliterate the flake scars. The fragment of Plate VIG seems to be a very similar but somewhat larger implement, however, the notch at its narrower end may be an intentional feature. One crudely flaked biface, roughly ovoid in shape and with battered edges, is probably a chopper. Several specimens could equally well be called choppers or unfinished knives.

Pecked-and Ground-stone Artifacts

One artifact, not figured, might be described as of polished stone. It is essentially a broad-based, leaf-shaped point about 6.2 centimeters long and 3.2 centimeters broad near the base. One side is completely polished, but on the other only the edges have been ground, which gives the implement an unfinished appearance. The raw material was a thin flake of greenstone. One corner of the base is broken. The general shape and size suggest the groundslate harpoon end blades of other parts of the Eskimo area, but this resemblance may be coincidental. As an artifact type, it is certainly unique at Krugloi Point. The specimen was found in Excavation Unit 4W at the 4-to-5-foot level.

Partial grinding of chipped-stone tools has been mentioned above, particularly in the case of specimens thought to be planing adzes or chisels.

Four examples of hemispherical lamps probably made from beach cobbles were found in Excavation Unit 4. Their proveniences are: West Section, 0-1 feet (Plate XXIIA); with Feature 3 (Plate XXIIC); Middle Section, 2-3 feet (Plate XXIID); and East Section, 2-3 feet (Plate XXIIE). All exhibit the same basic pattern—a flattened hemisphere produced by pecking a shallow basin out of a probably more-or-less-flat side of a cobblestone. The specimen illustrated as Plate XXIIA appears to have been pecked over the sides and bottom as well, and the lamp of Plate XXIIC has pecking scars on the bottom. Basins range in maximum depth from about 1.5 to nearly 3.0 centimeters. Maximum external diameters range from about 15 to 21 centimeters. All are soot blackened on a part of the basin wall and the adjacent lip and exterior wall. The material is in every case graywacke, a sedimentary rock composed of finegrained volcanic detritus.

Plate XXIIB illustrates what might be called, loosely, a vessel or lamp made by pecking a basin into a waterworn tabular fragment of graywacke. The basin is shallow, crudely formed, and shows no trace of soot blackening. It is possible that the specimen is some sort of anvil stone. Its provenience is Excavation Unit 4, West Section, 4-5 feet. A final example of the lamp or vessel category is a fragment of basalt showing part of a neatly pecked basin from the 3-to-4-foot level of the West Section of Excavation Unit 4.

A distinctive form of doubtful function is represented by a carefully shaped implement of coarse-grained basalt. Its shape and size are quite close to that of an elliptical cake of soap. Dimensions are 11.5 centimeters on the long axis, 5.5 centimeters on the short axis, and 3.2 centimeters in thickness. The top and bottom are very slightly convex along the long axis, and the sides are essentially straight or very slightly convex and vertical. A barely perceptible shallow, polished groove extends along the long axis on the top, and the bottom bears fine-scratched grooves and in its center an area of pecking scars as if the stone had served as an anvil. I would suppose that the specimen is a combination polisher, abrader, and anvil stone, although I have no explanation of why so humble an implement should be so neatly finished. It resembles fairly closely the paint grinders of Jochelson (1925, P. 17, 9, and 22). The specimen was found in Excavation Unit 1, Upper Level.

A very common sort of artifact in the pecked-stone class is a beach cobble modified by grooves, pits, or both to serve as a fishing line sinker or hammerstone. Modified cobbles total 123 specimens, about 15 per cent of all the artifacts found. With the exception of Excavation Unit 1, they are nearly ubiquitous, although there does appear to be a slight tendency toward occurrence in groups rather than an even scatter. The total absence of the class from Excavation Unit 1 is puzzling, as on statistical grounds one would expect some 13 or 14 examples. I hesitate to ascribe the absence to a real cultural difference, as it is extraordinarily difficult to suppose that the people of the upper village did not use hammerstones or line sinkers.

The most plentiful type of modified cobble is the line sinker made by pecking grooves at both ends of the major axis of the stone to make possible a secure lashing. The grooves are perpendicular to the flatter faces of the cobble. Range of maximum diameters of these ovoid stones is 5.0 to 19.5 centimeters with a mean on the order of 100 millimeters. Our collection has a total of 92 end-grooved sinkers, of which 66 show no definite modification other than the pecked end grooves (a few specimens have a groove at one end only) although in some cases the ends are battered through use as a hammerstone. The specimens illustrated by Heizer (1956, Plate 29g) and Jochelson (1925, Plate 17, nos. 14, 15, and 21) represent the type well. Twenty-one of the end-grooved stones bear pits on one or, more commonly, both faces and have battered ends indicating use as hammerstones. In view of the abundant beach cobbles at the site, I have no ready explanation for this economical double use. Presumably the use as line sinker is prior, that is, line sinkers were modified to use as hammerstones rather than the reverse, as there is no point in pecking grooves on the working ends of hammerstones. Moreover, in some cases, the battering has all but obliterated part of the end groove.

In addition to this clear type of sinker or sinker-hammerstone, a few specimens have other types of grooving. One is a large cobblestone completely encircled by a groove on the long axis; the major axis is about 20.0 centimeters, the minor axis about 18.5 centimeters. Both the style of grooving and the size place this stone outside the ordinary category of line sinkers. This specimen was a surface find on the beach. One other stone has a similar encircling groove, also on the long axis, but it is much smaller, no more than 5.9 centimeters on the long axis. This specimen came from Excavation Unit 4, Middle Section, below 7 feet. Another specimen having the same provenience is an elongated stone (long axis, 22.0 centimeters, short axis, about 9.5 centimeters) almost girdled around the short axis by four pecked pits, two of which are connected by a groove. In addition to this modification, a lightly pecked groove extends along the long axis on one face nearly to the end of the stone. One end of this stone is heavily battered, the other somewhat less so. A generally similar, but slightly smaller, specimen also came from the same provenience unit. From a foot above (Excavation Unit 4, Middle Section, 6-7 foot level), came a double-pitted hammerstone with four short parallel grooves on one face and edge and eight similar grooves on the same face and the adjacent edge. Another fragment (Excavation Unit 4, Middle Section, 5-6 feet) has grooves apparently nearly encircling the stone on both the major and minor axes. An elongated double-pitted hammerstone has traces of a shallow, probably unfinished, groove encircling the stone in the plane of the short axis and intersecting the pits and also a groove in the plane of the long axis on one face. This specimen was found in Excavation Unit 4, West Section, 4 to 5 feet.

The remaining 23 specimens are simply hammerstones, usually with pits on both faces but occasionally having only one pit. Their shape is characteristically ovoid, and nearly all specimens have battered ends. Some specimens have battered areas on the edges as well, and in one case the entire periphery seems to have been used for hammering. Maximum length ranges from about 10

ARTIFACTS, FAUNA, AND FLORA

to 18 centimeters. Variation in weight is, of course, much more pronounced. Most of the hammers came from the lower levels of Excavation Unit 4, although two were found in Excavation Unit 2. I have commented above on the absence of modified cobbles of any kind from Excavation Unit 1.

The material for modified cobblestones seems to exhibit about the same range for both hammerstones and line sinkers. Identified specimens include andesite and trachyte porphyry, diorite, tuff, felsite, conglomerate or sandstone (graywacke?), and granite.

Plate XXIXC illustrates a final stone specimen, a waterworn piece of fossil coral drilled through with a tapering hole 11 millimeters in diameter at the larger end. Probably the specimen is the socket piece for a bow drill. The provenience is Excavation Unit 4, Middle Section, 2-3 feet. No other examples of fossil coral were seen at Krugloi Point, and the material may be evidence of trade.

Bone and Teeth Artifacts

A total of 289 artifacts of bone and teeth was found at Krugloi Point. The specimens vary from fragments of neatly made barbed points to no more than fragments of bones showing evidence of hacking or sawing and a few split or otherwise broken teeth. A nearly complete range is illustrated on Plates XXIII-XXXI. Specimens were found in every excavation unit except the nearly barren Unit 3. Distribution by gross provenience units adjusted for volume does not differ strikingly from that of all artifacts, although there is some tendency for the class to be underrepresented in Unit 4, Middle Section, and overrepresented in Unit 4, West Section, relative to other artifacts. The counts are: Excavation Unit 1, Upper, 9 specimens; Unit 1, Lower, 13 specimens; Unit 2, 16 specimens; Unit 3, 0 specimens; Unit 4E and Feature 1, 82 specimens; Unit 4M, 0-3 feet, 26 specimens; Unit 4M, below 3 feet, 40 specimens; Unit 4W, 0-3 feet, 39 specimens; and Unit 4W, below 3 feet, 60 specimens. Provenience is unknown for 4 specimens.

After consultation with various authoritative reports on Aleutian and other Eskimo material culture and archaeology, I am still somewhat uncertain about functional categories for most of the specimens. This haziness results from the usually fragmentary condition of the specimens and scarcity of information on the western Aleutians rather than from defects in the sources consulted. Nearly all of the relatively complete and distinctive forms are figured.

Projectiles.—Descriptions of Eskimo and Aleut material culture abound in such interesting terms as lances; leisters; bird darts; seal, sea otter, and sea lion darts; toggle harpoons; and arrows. Better endowed investigators also speak of socket pieces, foreshafts, harpoon points, end blades, and even finger rests. Since the Krugloi Point people obviously obtained their living from the sea, one can expect cognate items in our collections, but this expectation is by no means completely fulfilled. The Krugloi Point bone industry is comparatively simple or impoverished from the standpoint of both the number of types present and the complexity of the types which did occur.

Nine specimens, all fragmentary, comprise the class of barbed bone points. They are illustrated as Plate XXIIIA, B, C, H, I, and J and plate XXIVE, F, and G. The specimen of Plate XXIII-I is the only bilaterally barbed point. Its tip is broken off, and its transverse section is a flattened ellipse. Property marks or decoration are absent. The specimen is 95 millimeters long, and it was found in Unit 4, Middle Section, below 7 feet. Presumably it is a dart head for sea mammal hunting.

Plate XXIIIA, B, H, and J are slender unilaterally barbed points. Plate XXIIIJ (Unit 4, West Section, 1-2 feet) appears to be complete except for a very small missing portion of the point and a broken base. It is nearly round in transverse section, and has 4 delicately incised barbs. Plate XXIIIH (Unit 4, West Section, 3-4 feet) is a similar but larger point. Only 2 barbs are present on the remaining fragment, but enough of the base is preserved to show a single-bevel hafting arrangement. When the point is viewed with the bevel uppermost (as in the illustration), the barbs are to the right. Plate XXIIIB (Unit 4, West Section 3-4 feet) is a tip fragment with 2 bolder barbs; its transverse section is a flattened ellipse. Plate XXIIIA (Unit 4, West Section 3-4 feet) seems to be a similar type. Its tip has been cut off just below a barb, and there is one remaining complete barb. Two transverse property marks are present. The function of these slender barbed points is not clear to me; they could have been dart points, bird spear side prongs, or even arrow points, although the bow and arrow is thought to have been very rare, or absent, in the western Aleutians. The specimen of Plate XXIVF (Unit 4, West Section, 2-3 feet) probably belongs to the same functional class, although it is somewhat heavier, has the barbs cut in a slightly different manner, and is subrectangular in transverse section. The base of the point is cut off, and the tip is broken at the base of a second barb.

Plate XXIVG (Unit 4, West Section, 4-5 feet) is a fragment of a still heavier unilaterally barbed point, or foreshaft, with 2 barbs remaining. Its transverse section is a fat ellipse with a sharper edge on the barb side. It is made of cancellous bone, probably whale bone. Plate XXIIIC (Unit 4, Feature 1) is a tip fragment with one barb and a hacked and broken base. The tip is rounded off neatly and is obviously not intended to pierce anything. The transverse section seems to be basically circular. Plate XXIVE (Unit 4, Middle Section, 5-6 feet) also shows a specimen with a single barb; it is subrectangular in transverse section and has, on one side, a deep longitudinal groove beginning at the base of the barb and extending to the battered proximal end. The ends of the fragment have obviously been reshaped to convert the specimen into a wedge.

The only artifact with an end modified to receive a point is illustrated as Plate XXIVA (Unit 1, Lower). The modification consists of a scoop-shaped basin about 18 millimeters long made by cutting transversely a little less than half through the rod of bone and then removing most of the material between the cut and the square end so as to leave a thin wall. Presumably, the tang of a stone point was placed in the basin and secured by lashing. On the reverse side, about 1 millimeter from the squared end, is a shallow transverse groove which I take to be a stop for the lashing. Both sides bear diagonal incised lines of the type usually called property marks. The transverse section is a pointed ellipse, approximately football-shaped, and there is no evidence of barbing. Since the artifact is broken off about 58 millimeters from its distal end, it is impossible to say anything about articulation with a shaft.

The specimens of Plate XXIVB, C, and D (Unit 4, West Section, 6-8 feet; 4W, 5-6 feet; and 4, substratum) seems to be small dart points with battered ends, but strictly speaking XXIVD does not belong in this discussion at all because it is made of wood. All 3 specimens are subrectangular in transverse section.

Pointed bone objects.--This obscure and none too accurate heading refers to 35 artifacts and fragments of artifacts illustrated as Plate XXIVH and I, Plate XXVIC-H, and Plate XXVII. The function, or functions, of these artifacts is not at all clear to us, but the most likely explanations would appear to be foreshafts, dart prongs, or arrow points. The foreshaft explanation is weakened, perhaps fatally, by the complete absence of socketed points which would fit on such foreshafts. From a descriptive point of view, one can divide the specimens into two classes, those with conical tangs and those with beveled tangs.

Examples of the conical-tanged class are shown on Plate XXIVH and I and Plate XXVIIA-E. The specimens of Plate XXIV are heavier and broader than the other members of the class. They are subrectangular in transverse section with dense outer bone on

one surface and cancellous bone on the other. Specimen XXIVH is
perforated with a biconical drilled hole, and its tip is slightly compressed as if it had been inserted into a socket. Specimen XXIVH
is from Unit 4, West Section, 3-4 feet, and XXIV-I from Unit 4,
Middle Section, below 7 feet. The five specimens of Plate XXVII
give an idea of the range in form and size of the remaining examples. The long tangs of XXVIIB and C show longitudinal ground
facets, although they are essentially circular in transverse section.
The tips of XXVIIA and B are broken. Three fragments are not illustrated; one of them is similar in shape to XXVIID and E but is
only 38 millimeters long. The distinctively shaped specimen
XXVIIC and a fragment probably belonging to the class are from
the lower level of Unit 1. The remaining specimens are from various sections and levels of Unit 4.

More-or-less pointed artifacts with beveled tangs are illustrated by Plates XXVIC-H and XXVIIF-I. These artifacts have
rounded tips and very long, gently tapering tangs formed by a single bevel. Specimens XXVIIG and H have a small shoulder on the
beveled end and on the face opposite to the bevel, presumably to
prevent the lashing from slipping. All are approximately round in
transverse section above the beveled part. The specimen of Plate
XXVIIF has a diagonal cut above the bevel that looks like the beginning of a barb. If this is indeed a barb, it is open toward the
"point" rather than the beveled end. Range in size is covered adequately by the illustrations. Nine of the 10 illustrated artifacts
come from various sections and all levels of Unit 4, and 1 specimen was found in the lower level of Unit 1. In addition to the illustrated specimens, there are 6 fragments showing a single bevel
like that of the complete examples. One of these came from Unit 2,
1 from Unit 1, and the remaining 4 from Unit 4.

Nine tip fragments were found which could have come from
either the conical or the beveled-tang classes or possibly from
some quite different sort of artifact. The tips are rounded rather
than brought to a sharp point in most cases (no observation could
be made on two specimens owing to battered tips), and on 2 specimens the base is cut and broken rather than simply broken off.

Wedges.--Wedges are illustrated as Plate XXVD and F-J. General
shape and battered heads make the functional identification certain.
Forty-four examples were found, of which 40 were complete. They
were quite evenly distributed over the various excavation units and
in the levels of Unit 4. The actual distribution is: Unit 1, Upper,
3 wedges; Unit 1, Lower, 2; Unit 2, 4; Unit 3, 0; Unit 4, Upper, 18;
and Unit 4 Lower (below 3 feet), 17 wedges. One barbed point that

had been reworked into a wedge has been described above. One of the wedges (Plate XXVG) is ivory, probably whale tooth. The rest are of bone, and the size and curvature suggests that whale rib was a favored raw material. The basic form is simple—when viewed from the top, the sides are usually straight and parallel, and when viewed from the side the top and bottom are parallel or more rarely converge from the head to the thin end. One specimen is plano convex in side view. The transverse section is most often subrectangular (width usually exceeds thickness), but plano-convex sections occur. The quadrilateral section is the result of grinding or splitting a facet on top, bottom, and the sides. Range in length is from 2.9 to 13.1 centimeters and in width from 1.2 to 4.7 centimeters. More than half of the specimens have a width- length ratio of less than .40, and width does not increase proportionately in the longer specimens. Apparently no particular advantage was attributed to a width of more than about 4 centimeters regardless of the absolute length of the tool. The very short and relatively wide specimens (Plate XXV-I, for example) were probably reduced in length by use through repeated battering of the head and reshaping of the thin end. The unusually shaped specimen of Plate XXV-I is probably a reworked fragment of some other type of tool. The thin ends were formed by hacking and grinding intersecting bevels on top and bottom. The bevels meet at an angle of about 30 degrees. Several specimens were clearly made from blanks removed from large bones by a grooving and splitting process. Most of such grooves were cut from the denser outer surface toward the inner, cancellous bone, but a few specimens were grooved from both sides. Many wedges, however, were evidently made from smaller bones which already possessed a suitable transverse section.

Flakers.—Two examples of the baculum flaker were found. They are illustrated as Plate XXIXA and D. The larger specimen is presumably sea lion, and the smaller is probably seal. Both specimens have broken tips. The specimen of Plate XXIXA was found in Unit 4, Middle Section, 6-7 feet, and that of Plate XXIXD in Unit 4, West Section, 7-8 feet. Rib flakers are illustrated as Plate XXVA and B. The tips are smooth and were probably finished by grinding. The single-tipped specimen has a roughly squared broken base, but it is probably not an accidental break. Specimen XXVA was found in Unit 4, West Section, 7-8 feet, and specimen XXVB in Unit 4, Middle Section, below 7 feet. A third specimen also from Unit 4, Middle Section, below 7 feet, is probably a flaker, but it was made from a straight section of some heavy bone and is plano-convex rather than rectangular in transverse section.

Drill sockets.--Three specimens are thought to be socket pieces for the ends of bow drills. One (Plate XXIXC), made from fossil coral, has been discussed above. The other two (Plate XXIXE and F) are roughly rectangular pieces of heavy bone, probably whale, with holes drilled from one side. When viewed in radial section, the holes have rounded tops. The hole has perforated specimen XXIXE, and a second socket has been started adjacent to the first. On specimen XXIXF, the socket has not penetrated deeply enough to break through the opposite side of the bone. Specimen XXIXE was found in Unit 4, East Section, in the 2-3-foot level. Specimen XXIXF is from Unit 4, Middle Section, 2-3 feet.

Tooth ornaments.--Worked teeth are illustrated as Plate XXIII, D-G and K-L. Most of the specimens (14) came from Feature 1, Unit 4, and 12 of them were judged to be associated with Burial 4 of Feature 1. Ten of these are small sea lion teeth fitted with an encircling groove at one end or the other (Plate XXIIIF-G), and 2 are larger split sea lion teeth perforated near the proximal end of the type illustrated by Plate XXIIIK. We suppose that they formed a necklace or were attached to a garment. The specimen of Plate XXIIID is an imitation in bone of a large grooved tooth. It was found unassociated in the pit fill of Feature 1, as was specimen XXIIIK. Specimen XXIIIE lay beside the skull of Burial 6 in Feature 1. Four specimens of tooth ornaments came from the upper foot of Unit 4, Middle Section, and may have been displaced from Feature 1. One is a large split and perforated tooth like that shown on Plate XXIIIK. Two are large grooved specimens very much like Plate XXIIID. The fourth is an unidentified tooth with a notch hacked into it near its base. The final example is that of Plate XXIIIL. The inclusion of this specimen in the category of ornaments is questionable, although it could have served some decorative purpose. It is a slender, highly polished bar of ivory with shallow grooves across either end on one side. Viewed from the side, it has a slightly plano-convex appearance with the grooves on the convex side. The specimen was found in Unit 4, East Section, in the 2-3-foot level.

Worked bird bone.--Specimens of modified bird bone are shown in Plate XXIXB and in Plate XXX. The major classes appear to be sliver needles (Plate XXXB-E, J, and K) and awls or awl-like tools from whole bones (Plate XXXA and F-I). There are, in addition, the drilled bone of Plate XXIXB and several cut sections of bone which probably represent unfinished artifacts or discarded sections of bone.

Eighteen sliver needles were found, all from Excavation Unit 4.

Ten of these came from the 2-to-4-foot level in the west section, and the remainder were scattered randomly. As the illustrations indicate, they are simply slivers of bone with a very sharp, polished piercing end. The upper end may be cut transversely, but more often it is simply broken. Two needles are pointed at both ends (Plate XXXB and J), and another (Plate XXXE) has halves of 2 drilled holes about a centimeter apart at its upper end. The needle has broken transversely through the upper hole.

Ten awls made from whole bones were found. All were from Unit 4, and 5 were from the 2-4-foot level in the west section. The points were formed by an oblique cut with subsequent grinding and polishing, and the tops may show the unmodified condyle or may be cut or broken through transversely. Three specimens have notching; in one case (Plate XXXF) there are opposing sets of 3 notches near the cut and broken upper end. A second specimen (Plate XXX-I) has 4 closely spaced notches about 4 centimeters above the pointed end. The third specimen has at least 3 sharp notches, almost barbs, on the broken pointed end, an opposing pair of wide shallow notches about 6 centimeters above the pointed end, and a single shallow notch about 1 centimeter below the opposed pair. The designation of all these artifacts as awls is questionable, as some have rounded ends rather than piercing points (Plate XXXA and H).

The remaining specimens are something of a miscellany. Plate XXIXB figures a large fragment of bird bone with 2 holes drilled through it. A slender 12 centimeter section cut at both ends has a deep longitudinal groove, probably a preparation for splitting the bone lengthwise. Two short sections of bone have still smaller sections of bone jammed inside them as if for safe keeping, and 1 of the splinter needles was thrust into a section of bird bone. Finally, there are 6 pieces which seem to be leftovers of artifact manufacture. Four are sections cut at one or both ends, another is partly cut and split, and the last is a fragment of a cut and split shaft.

Heavy bone tools.--Plate XXIB-E illustrates 4 heavy-pointed bone tools of the kind called root-diggers by Jochelson (1925, Plate 26 and p. 87). Two of the Krugloi Point specimens are double pointed, although the points are somewhat rounded. Specimen XXXIB has 1 sharpened point, but the other end is neatly rounded off. Specimen XXXID has a very low rectangular boss on one side in the middle of the implement (see illustration). All of these tools have polish and were evidently used extensively. Their transverse sections tend to be plano-convex or subrectangular, and they seem to have been made from heavy ribs. All show both dense outer bone and cancellous bone; the latter is on the convex side on 3 specimens.

Another sort of heavy tool is shown on Plate XXVIII. Here on 3 of these specimens a smoothed and thinned section of heavy rib has been rounded on one end. Specimens XXVIIIB, C, and D have a cut and broken end opposite to the rounded end, but XXVIIIA is ground off. The form of the shaped end of XXVIIIC is not clear owing to fracture, and its inclusion in the rounded-end class may be a mistake. These artifacts have a thinner, more rectangular transverse section than the pointed rib tools of the preceding paragraph.

A number of fragments of worked rib could have been derived from the root-digger and the rounded-end classes, and I judge that both were fairly common artifacts.

Other worked bone.--The artifact of Plate XXVE is a complete specimen of unknown function. It is a shaped section of rib which is subrectangular in transverse section and has rounded ends. One end is shaped as a step scarf. Plate XXVC illustrates a part of another artifact probably made from a rib and having a subrectangular transverse section. Again one end bears a step scarf or lashing step, but the opposite side also shows a flat bevel toward the step end.

A part of a large spatulate implement of whalebone is shown as Plate XXXIA. The complete artifact is 38 centimeters long. Most of one side is broken, but the remaining side does not taper. The unillustrated end is cut off squarely, and the opposite side consists of the smoothed and polished outer bone. The transverse section is concavo-convex--the implement was made by removing most of the cancellous bone so that the concave side is parallel to the rounded outer surface.

The only remaining nearly complete bone artifacts are 3 small pegs and a very large flat plate of whalebone. The pegs have rounded heads and taper slightly to rather blunt points; they range in length from 3.5 to 5 centimeters. The whalebone plate was probably approximately rectangular with dimensions of about 15 by 40 centimeters and a thickness of about 2 centimeters. It was made entirely from cancellous bone, and one side has been ground to a quite smooth finish.

The remaining bone specimens are industrial debris and fragments of various unidentified artifacts. Many of these are worked cylindrical fragments which could be parts of foreshafts, flakers, drill shafts, or other artifacts. Split bones with blunt points, small pieces of whalebone with some evidence of grinding, and other scraps bearing evidence of having been part of an artifact are quite common. Industrial debris is represented by whalebone plates from which segments have been detached by grooving and splitting (Plate XXIF and G), cut whale ribs, and other cut sections of bones of various kinds. Several whalebone fragments are charred. Eight fragments of whale teeth, often split longitudinally, probably belong in this category. There are 126 catalogued specimens in this class of unidentified artifact fragments and bone working debris.

Other materials.--Under this heading we have two modified bivalve shells and ten, supposedly, shaped pieces of wood. The shells have sections cut or broken away so as to leave one rather straight edge. One, from Unit 2, is a valve of the species *Saxidomes giganteus,* and the other, from Unit 4, East Section, 2-to-3-foot level, has been classified as *Ostria luxida.* What function (if any) these shells served is not clear to me. All of the wooden pieces were found in the muck at the base of the Unit 4 deposits. As I have described above, the unworked wood scraps from the muck were combined to make a radiocarbon sample, and the remaining pieces seem to have been worked. One has already been mentioned and is illustrated as Plate XXIVD. The remaining pieces are, for the most part, sticks of various diameters with cut, rounded, or pointed ends. In some cases I am not certain that driftwood abrasion is not responsible for the supposed shaping, but four specimens seem to be genuine artifact fragments. One is a 10-centimeter-long section of a neatly rounded shaft a little more than a centimeter in diameter. Two others have tapering round pointed ends rather like the root-diggers and subrectangular transverse sections. Both are broken off about 10 centimeters above the point, and their maximum widths are 1.5 and 2.5 centimeters. The fourth specimen is a tiny split fragment of a shaft with a rounded head. Another specimen is a thin, warped fragment which conceivably could be a part of a wooden tray. Three of the specimens are charred.

Faunal remains.--Unworked bones of mammals, birds, and fish were abundant in the refuse, and snail and bivalve shells were also common. The broken shells and spines of sea urchins, however, were probably the most important faunal component of the refuse as measured by volume. We collected our examples of bones and shells in a rather casual fashion, which undoubtedly means that we have anything but a random sample, and the only purpose our collection will serve is to indicate the presence of certain forms. All of the species noted are a part of the modern fauna and indicate, so far as they go, an economy indistinguishable from that of the early historic period.

With the exception of some fragments of human bone, mammal remains are exclusively those of sea animals. Whale bones were quite common, but our comparative material does not permit specific identification. Several skulls of fur seal were collected, but harbor seal is no more than possibly represented. Sea lion is clearly present; sea otter is probably represented. The human bones consist of a few fragments of long bones and a part of an infant's skull. I do not know whether they are the result of disturbed burials or whether they were deposited as fragments.

Bird bones in our collection include albatross (probably the short-tailed form), shearwater (probably *Puffinus*), cormorant, willow ptarmigan, gull (*Larus* sp.), alcids (probably *Uria*), and a goose of undetermined genus.

Shellfish other than sea urchins include *Acmaea mitra* and *A. pelta, Littorina sikana, Thais emarginata* and *T. canaliculata,* and *Podosesmus macroschisma,* as well as the worked specimens mentioned above of *Saxidomus giganteus* and *Ostrea lurida.*

Bones of true fish were abundant, but the specimens we collected are too thoroughly broken to permit identification. Some are from very large fish, probably halibut.

The human skeletal material has been loaned to William S. Laughlin of the University of Wisconsin for study as a part of his general investigation of human biology in the Aleutians.

CONCLUSION

The excavations at Krugloi Point were intended to furnish preliminary data on the character of prehistoric Aleut culture in the comparatively little-known and remote western end of the island chain. We hoped that our excavations would (1) provide information on the problem of dating the first occupation of the western Aleutians; (2) furnish good data for the study of interregional cultural variation in the Aleutians; (3) expose, at least in general outline, the nature of temporal change in western Aleutian culture; and (4) supply skeletal material of known cultural provenience to aid in the interpretation of the biological aspects of the peopling of the Aleutians and the subsequent development of the Aleutian population.

I have mentioned above the radiocarbon date of about 615 B. C. obtained from unworked fragments of wood found at the bottom of

CONCLUSION

the refuse mound of Excavation Unit 4. Although there is no certainty that the bottom of this particular refuse mound represents the first occupation of the Krugloi Point area, the date is, I think, the best estimate possible under the circumstances for the initial settlement. The date is a maximum, of course, because it estimates the time of death of various trees which ultimately drifted to Agattu, not the actual deposition of the wood in the refuse. The corrected date, which, for convenience, I shall take to be around 500 B.C. can be compared with Laughlin's date of about 1000 B.C. (Laughlin and Marsh, 1951, p. 81; Johnson, 1951, p. 11) for a deposit a meter above the base of the large refuse mound at Chaluka (Nikolski) on Umnak Island close to the eastern end of the Aleutians. A priority of something more than 500 years for Chaluka gives a comfortable span of time for the spread of the Aleuts from east to west, and the dates are mutually supporting. It would be incautious, however, to treat this pair of dates as anything more than suggestions in our present state of knowledge; there is no definite assurance that either represents the earliest settlement in its area. Published dates resulting from Bank's work at various sites in the eastern Aleutians (Crane, 1956; Crane and Griffin, 1959) are all somewhat later than those from Chaluka and Krugloi Point, a circumstance which does support the idea that the bottom of the Chaluka deposit is close to the beginning of settlement in the Aleutians.

Comparative material from Agattu is scarce indeed. The only collection known to me is that described in part by Hrdlička (1945, pp. 288-312, 411, 416, 431-86 *passim*) from his excavations at three sites in McDonald Cove some four airline miles to the southwest of Krugloi Point. The preliminary account does indicate a general similarity, however, especially in flaked-stone tools and in the relative scarcity of bone tools. Hrdlička recognized the special character of Agattu stone chipping and also suggested it might have been "conditioned by the easily worked local argilite [sic] materials" (1945, p. 312). The illustrated stone tools (Figs. 186-92) look quite familiar, but a fragment of a decorated stone lamp, a type not found at Krugloi Point, is reported (p. 305). The wedge decorated with bands of incised dots and circles and the animals effigies illustrated by Hrdlička in Fig. 203 and attributed to Agattu have no parallel at Krugloi Point. My general impression is one of a very similar culture, and this similarity extends to the burials figured and described and the large rectangular house on the upper part of one of the McDonald Cove sites.

In more general terms, the Krugloi Point sites are notable for a remarkably poor array of artifact types, especially types of bone tools. This point is brought home forcibly by even a cursory comparison with the artifact inventory of the Pacific Eskimo site of Uyak on Kodiak Island (Heizer, 1956), the generalized descriptions of Aleut culture and archaeology by Jochelson (1925), the reports of Laughlin (1952) and Laughlin and Marsh (1951 and 1956), and Bank (1953). Hurt (1950) observes in his comparison of the Krugloi Point material with a small collection of artifacts salvaged from airport building on Shemya, actually visible from Krugloi Point, that several types of artifacts from Shemya are not present at Krugloi Point. In this case, we can hardly plead remoteness to explain the impoverished condition of Krugloi Point, and there may be, as Hurt suggests, a time difference involved. Particularly notable absences from Krugloi Point are toggle harpoons, composite fishhooks, tanged chipped-stone knives, harpoon socket pieces, and polished-stone lamps. If the comparison were extended to details, especially in the case of bone tools, a very much longer list of absences could be prepared, but I think that enough has been said to establish the major point.

I have no ready explanation for this seeming distinctiveness of the bone industry. Perhaps the absence of so many bone types is, in part, a product of the general rarity of bone tools; additional excavation might expand the type list substantially. I can think of no plausible reason, however, for the quantitative deficiency in bone tools, so I have merely replaced one mystery by another in advancing the statistical argument. Moreover, Hrdlička reported the same condition at the McDonald Cove sites, and the problem must be considered something more than a one-site anomaly. I have no clear reason to suppose that the Agattu Aleut faced any unusual ecological or geographical circumstances which would account for a restricted tool inventory, which seems to leave as a final possibility the argument that the known Agattu sites represent an early population who brought an archaic and simple artifact inventory to the island and preserved it in relative isolation without much change for more than a millenium. This possibility will be discussed, together with the evidence for internal change at Krugloi Point.

Internal change has been discussed in some detail in the various sections on artifacts with the general conclusion that there is no indubitable evidence of difference between the stratigraphic units of Excavation Unit 4 or between the excavation units, although a suspicion of relative lateness for the upper site was mentioned. This interpretation is a positive one in the sense that all of the analysis units were generally similar, but it is by no means a prediction or claim that no cultural changes took place over the time

CONCLUSION

span sampled by our excavations. On the contrary, there must have been quantitative and qualitative changes over the 1,500 years or more, and I would expect that more extensive excavations would reveal their nature. On the other hand, I judge that our digging was sufficiently extensive to warrant an interpretation of relative stability and distinctiveness, particularly in the chipped-stone industry. On balance, I am inclined to favor the view that the early Aleuts did bring a simple artifact inventory to Agattu and that subsequent development was largely a matter of the rapid evolution of a distinctive chipped-stone industry stemming from the special local resources. It may be that a number of new elements were introduced to Agattu at a later date than is represented at Krugloi Point as is suggested by the Shemya material, but as yet there is no direct evidence of this.

Under these particular circumstances, I can do very little in the way of comparing and contrasting the Krugloi Point sequence with the trends indicated by Quimby (1948), Laughlin and Marsh (1951, 1956), Laughlin (1952), and Bank (1953). Most of the artifact types or art styles these authors employ are either absent or rare in our collection, and there is little possibility of quantitative comparison. In fact, as I have suggested above, there are some kinds of artifacts absent at Krugloi Point which ought to be present in some form in any Aleut culture at any time. Examples of these artifacts are various types of bone harpoons (including the toggling variety) and darts. Further, the existing sequences have been worked out primarily in the eastern Aleutians hundreds of miles from Agattu, and one would not expect identity in all details. Certainly, the Krugloi Point material does not refute or suggest any substantial modifications of current views. Its simple, rather archaic flavor is in keeping with the idea that the main stream of diffusion was from the Alaska Peninsula westward.

REFERENCES CITED

Bank, Theodore P., II
    1953 Cultural Succession in the Aleutians. Amer. Antiq., Vol. 19, No. 1, pp. 40-49. Salt Lake City: University of Utah.

Collins, Henry D., Jr., Clark, Austin H., and Walker, Egbert H.
    1945 The Aleutian Islands: Their People and Natural History. Smithsonian Institution War Background Studies No. 21 (Publ. 3775). Washington, D. C.

Crane, H. R.
    1956 University of Michigan Radiocarbon Dates I. Science, Vol. 124, No. 3224, pp. 664-72.

Crane, H. R., and Griffin, James B.
    1959 University of Michigan Radiocarbon Dates IV. Amer. J. Sci. Radiocarbon Suppl., Vol. I, pp. 173-98.

Heizer, Robert F.
    1956 Archaeology of the Uyak Site, Kodiak Island, Alaska. Univ. Cal., Anthropol. Records, Vol. 17, No. 1.

Hrdlička, Aleš
    1945 The Aleutian and Commander Islands and Their Inhabitants. Philadelphia: The Wistar Institute of Anatomy and Biology.

Hurt, Wesley R., Jr.
    1950 Artifacts From Shemya, Aleutian Islands. Amer. Antiq., Vol. 16, No. 1, p. 69. Salt Lake City: University of Utah.

Jochelson, Waldemar
    1925 Archaeological Investigations in the Aleutian Islands. Carnegie Institutions of Washington, Publ. 367. Washington, D. C.

Johnson, Frederick (ed.)
    1951 Radiocarbon Dating. Mem. Soc. Amer. Archaeol., No. 8.

Laughlin, William S.
    1952 The Aleut-Eskimo Community, Anthropol. Papers of the Univ. Alaska, Vol. 1, No. 1, pp. 25-46. College, Alaska

Laughlin, William S. and Marsh, Gordon H.
    1951 A New View of the History of the Aleutians. Arctic, J. of the Arctic Inst. of North America, Vol. 4, No. 2, pp. 75-88.

―――――
    1954 The Lamellar Flake Manufacturing Site on Anangula Island in the Aleutians. Amer. Antiq., Vol. 20, No. 1, pp. 27-39. Salt Lake City: University of Utah.

REFERENCES

Laughlin, William S. and Marsh, Gordon H.
    1956   Trends in Aleutian Chipped Stone Artifacts. Anthropol. Papers of the Univ. Alaska, Vol. 5, No. 1, pp. 5-22. College, Alaska.

Quimby, George I.
    1948   Prehistoric Art of the Aleutian Islands. Chicago Mus. Nat. Hist. Fieldiana: Anthropol., Vol. 36, No. 3, pp. 77-92.

Sharp, Robert P.
    1946   Notes on the Geology of Agattu, an Aleutian Island. J. Geol., Vol. 54, No. 3, pp. 193-99.

Spaulding, Albert C.
    1953   The Current Status of Aleutian Archaeology. *In* Asia and North America: Transpacific Contacts (assembled by Marian W. Smith). Mem. Soc. Amer. Archaeol., No. 9, Amer. Antiq., Vol. 18, No. 3, Pt. 2, pp. 29-31. Salt Lake City: University of Utah.

EXPLANATION OF PLATE LEGENDS

University of Michigan Museum of Anthropology catalogue numbers, provenience, and references to duplicate illustrations are listed for artifacts. Excavation units are numbered from 1 to 4. Excavation Unit 4 has three planimetric divisions: the east (E), middle (M), and west (W) sections, and numbered features (Fea. 1, Fea. 2, and so on). Artifacts from Excavation Unit 1 are segregated in upper (U) and lower (L) levels, and artifacts from Excavation Unit 4 are segregated in arbitrary 1-foot layers (0-1, 1-2, and so on). Artifacts figured in two plates have the plate and figure number of the duplicate listed. For example, the artifact figured as Plate VID has the catalogue number 31481, comes from Excavation Unit 4, west section, 2-to-3-foot level, and is also illustrated as Plate IXB. Its legend is D:31481, 4W, 2-3 (IXB).

PLATE I

Fig. 1. Upper site. Clearing for Excavation Unit 1 in right middle ground. UMMA Neg. 11095.

Fig. 2. Excavation Unit 1 completed. UMMA Neg. 11096.

PLATE II

Fig. 1. Site area, looking east. Part of upper site in left foreground; lower site is point of dark vegetation extending inland in right middle ground. UMMA Neg. 11601.

Fig. 2. Edge of site and Excavation Unit 4 refuse mound, looking southeast. UMMA Neg. 11602.

PLATE III

Fig. 1. Feature 1, Excavation Unit 4, partly cleared. Looking west. UMMA Neg. 11099.

Fig. 2. Feature 4, Excavation Unit 4, looking northeast. UMMA Neg. 11100.

PLATE IV

Fig. 1. Feature 1, Excavation Unit 4, lower bones exposed. Looking southwest. UMMA Neg. 11097.

Fig. 2. South wall, Excavation Unit 4. UMMA Neg. 11098.

PLATE V

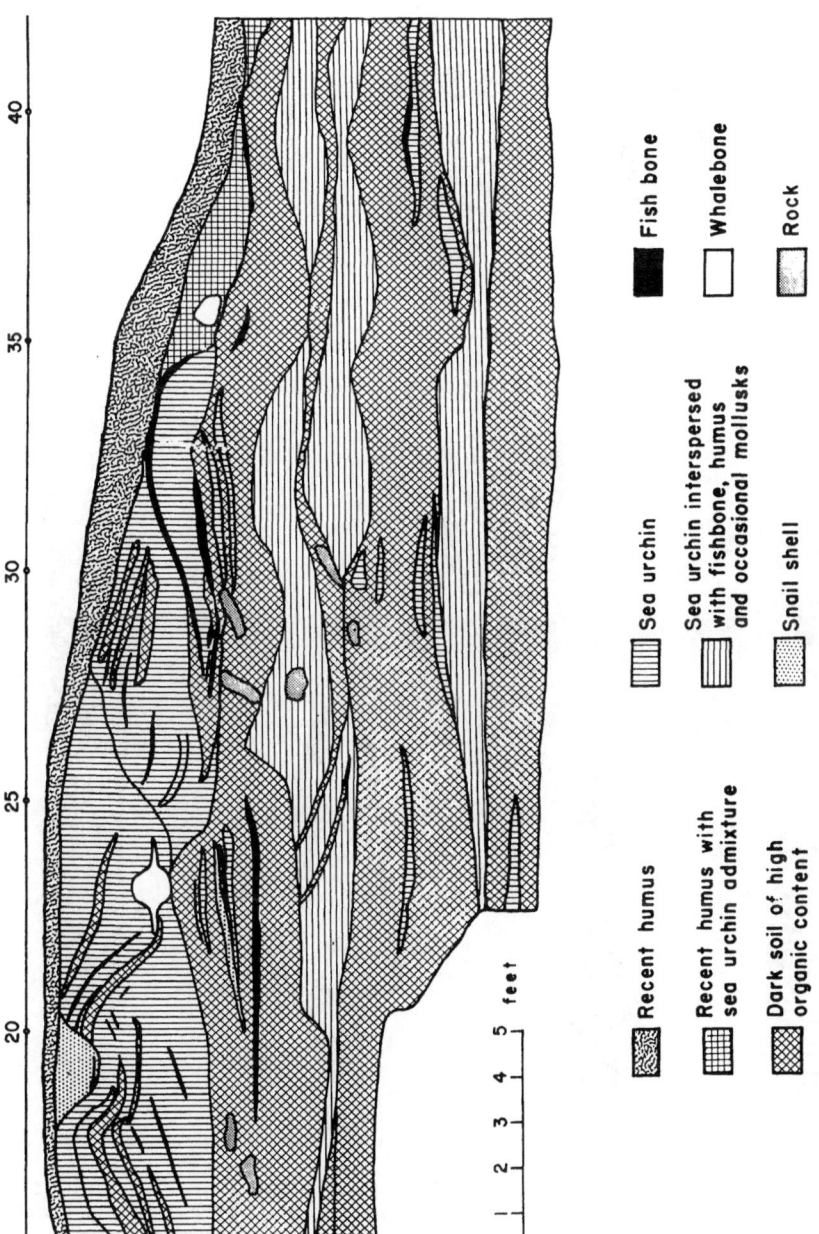

Excavation Unit 4. Middle and west sections of south wall.

PLATE VI

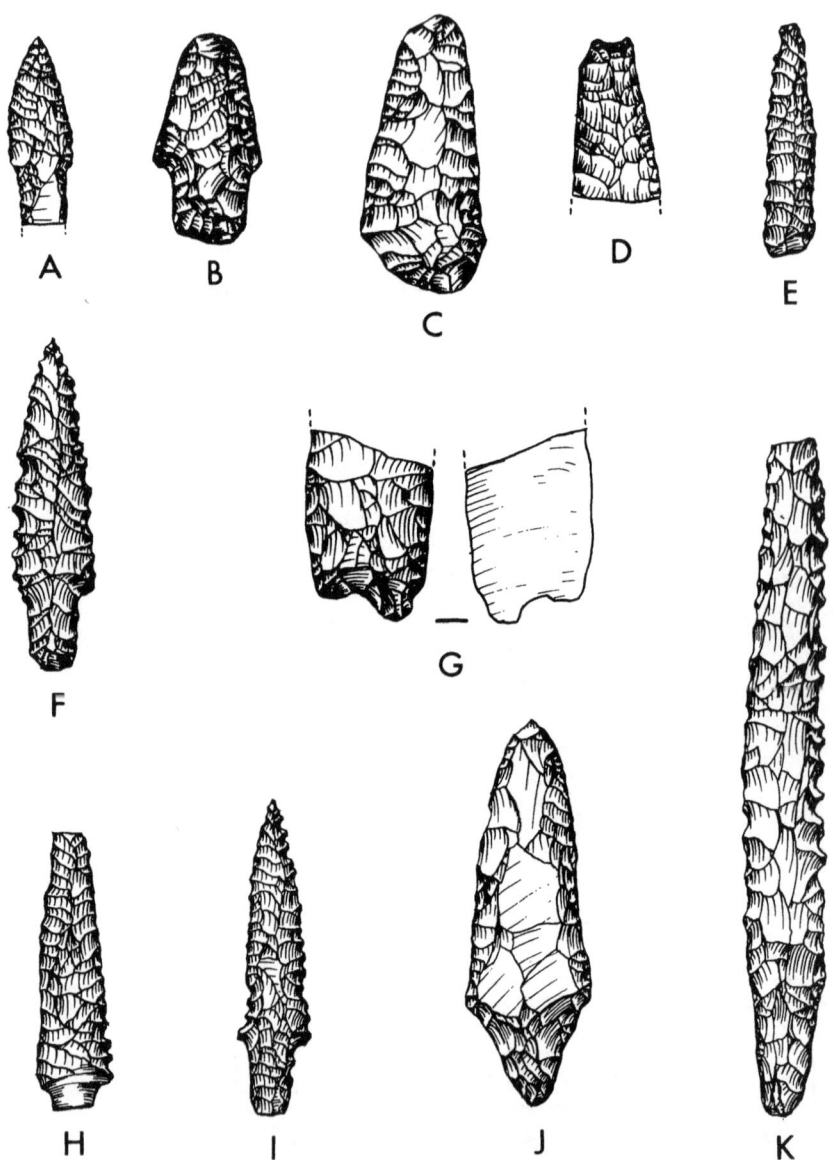

Projectile points, blades, and drills. Specimen K is 15.5 cm long.
A:32756, 4M, 5-6 (XF); B:32652, 1U (XIIB); C:32648, 1L (XIIIG); D:31481, 4W, 2-3 (IXB); E:32690, 4W, 1-2 (XC); F:32713, 4E, 3-4 (XIH); G:31481, 4W, 2-3 (XVIIIE); H:32648, 1L (XIF); I:32661, 2· (XA); J:32685, 4M, 1-2 (XIIIE); K:32799, 4, Fea. 1 (IXG).

PLATE VII

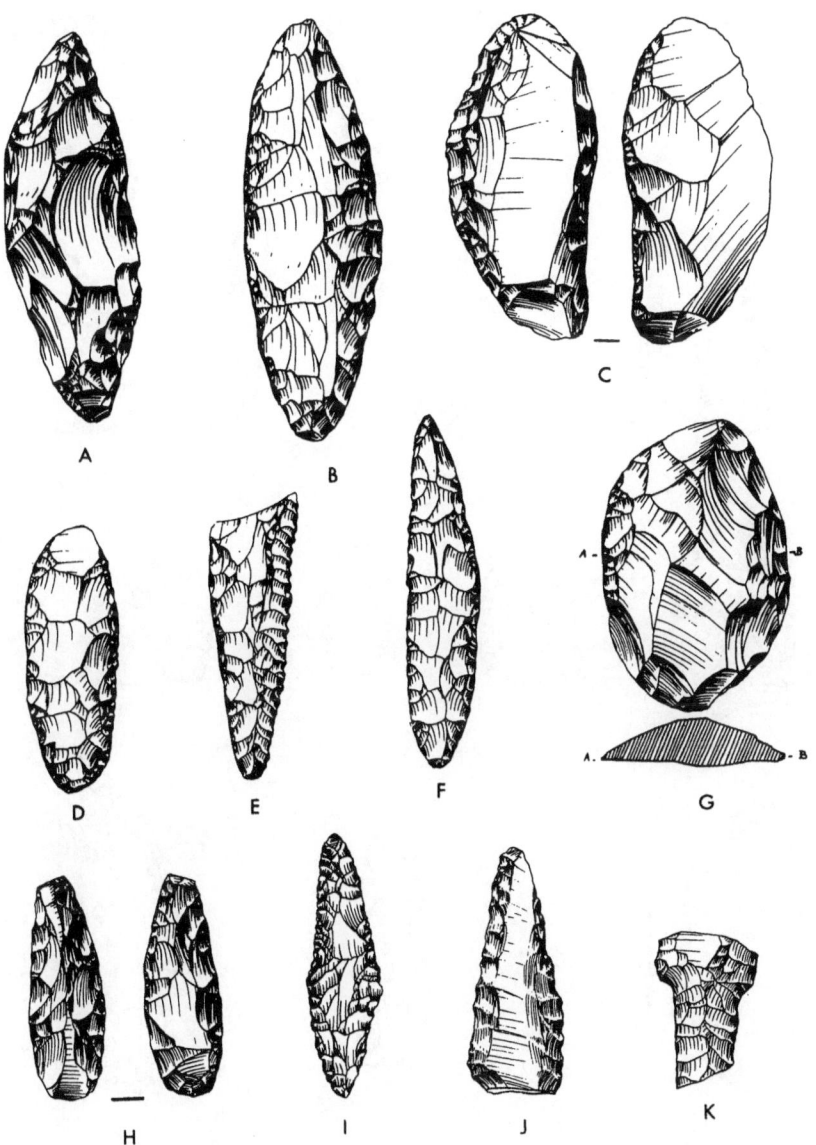

Bifacial blades. Specimen B is 16.4 cm long. A:32687, 4M, 1-2 (XXIB); B:31481, 4W, 2-3 (XVIIE); C:32725, 4W, 3-4 (XVIID); D:32720, 4M, 3-4 (XVA); E:32799, 4, Fea. 1 (XVIB); F:32720, 4M, 3-4 (XVID); G:32648, 1L (XXIA); H:32694, 4E, 2-3 (XVIIID); I:32706, 4M, 2-3 (IXE); J:32737, 4M, 4-5 (XVIIB); K:32750, 4W, 4-5 (IXD).

PLATE VIII

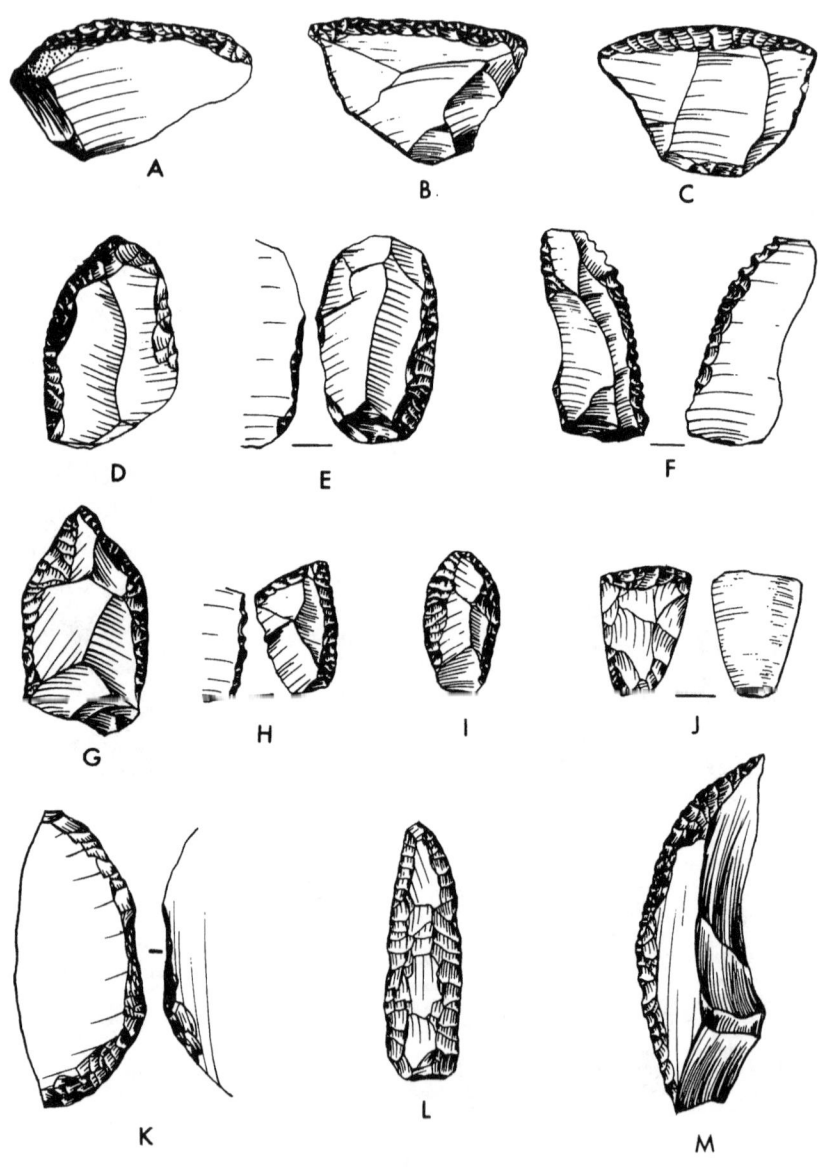

Knife, scrapers, adze, and serrated flake. Specimen M is 12.1 cm long. A:32687, 4M, 1-2 (XVC); B:32725, 4W, 3-4 (XIVC); C:32666, 4M, 0-1 (XIVB); D:31481, 4W, 2-3 (XIXB); E:32691, 4W, 1-2 (XIXA); F:32686, 4M, 1-2 (XIXG); G:32687, 4M, 1-2 (XIXE); H:32666, 4M, 0-1 (XIXC); I:32745, 4W, 4-5 (XIXD); J:32674, 4E, 0-1 (XVIIIA); K:32687, 4M, 1-2 (XVE); L:32737, 4M, 4-5 (XVIIA); M:32687, 4M, 1-2 (XXB).

PLATE IX

Projectile points. Specimen G is 15.5 cm long. A:32695, 4E, 2-3; B:31481, 4W, 2-3 (VID); C:32695, 4E, 2-3; D:32750, 4W, 4-5 (VIIK); E:32706, 4M, 2-3 (VII-I); F:32683, 4M, 1-2; G:32799, 4, Fea. 1 (VIK). UMMA Neg. 11081.

PLATE X

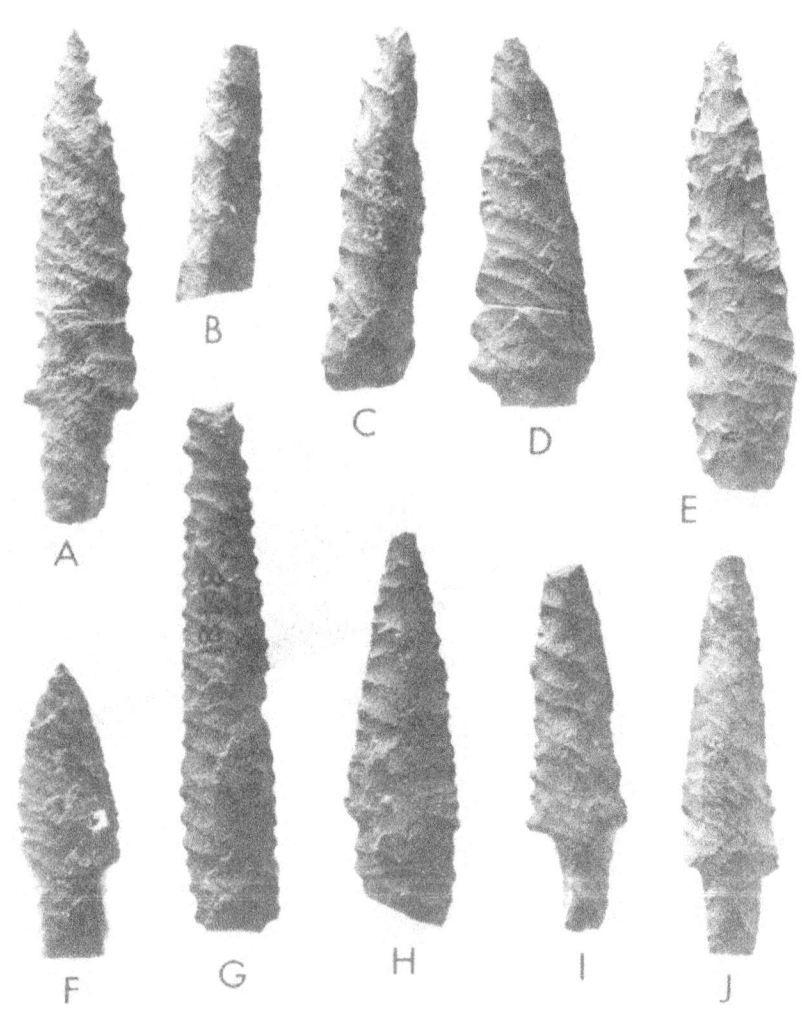

Projectile points and drill. Specimen G is 7.8 cm long. A:32661, 2 (VI-I); B:31481, 4W, 2-3; C:32690, 4W, 1-2 (VIE); D:32724, 4W, 3-4; E:31481, 4W, 2-3; F:32756, 4M, 5-6 (VIA); G:31481, 4W, 2-3; H:32661, 2; I:32724, 4W, 3-4; J:32695, 4E, 2-3. UMMA Neg. 11080.

PLATE XI

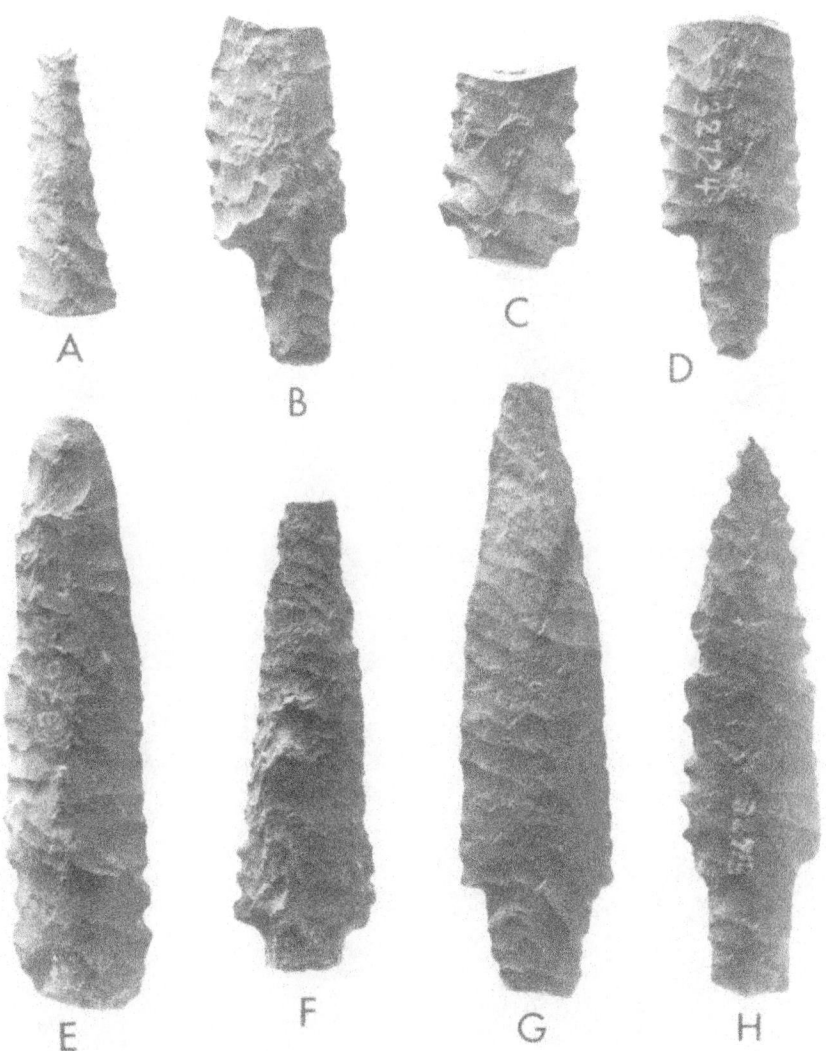

Projectile points. Specimen E is 8.2 cm long. A:32668, 4M, 0-1; B:32695, 4E, 2-3; C:32695, 4E, 2-3; D:32724, 4W, 3-4; E:32648, 1L; F:32648, 1L (VIH); G:32648, 1L; H:32713, 4E, 3-4 (VIF). UMMA Neg. 11079.

PLATE XII

Projectile points. Specimen G is 7.7 cm long. A:32661, 2; B:32652, 1U (VIB); C:32737, 4M, 4-5; D:32695, 4E, 2-3; E:32690, 4W, 1-2; F:32657, 2; G:32788, 4; H:32695, 4E, 2-3. UMMA Neg. 11069.

PLATE XIII

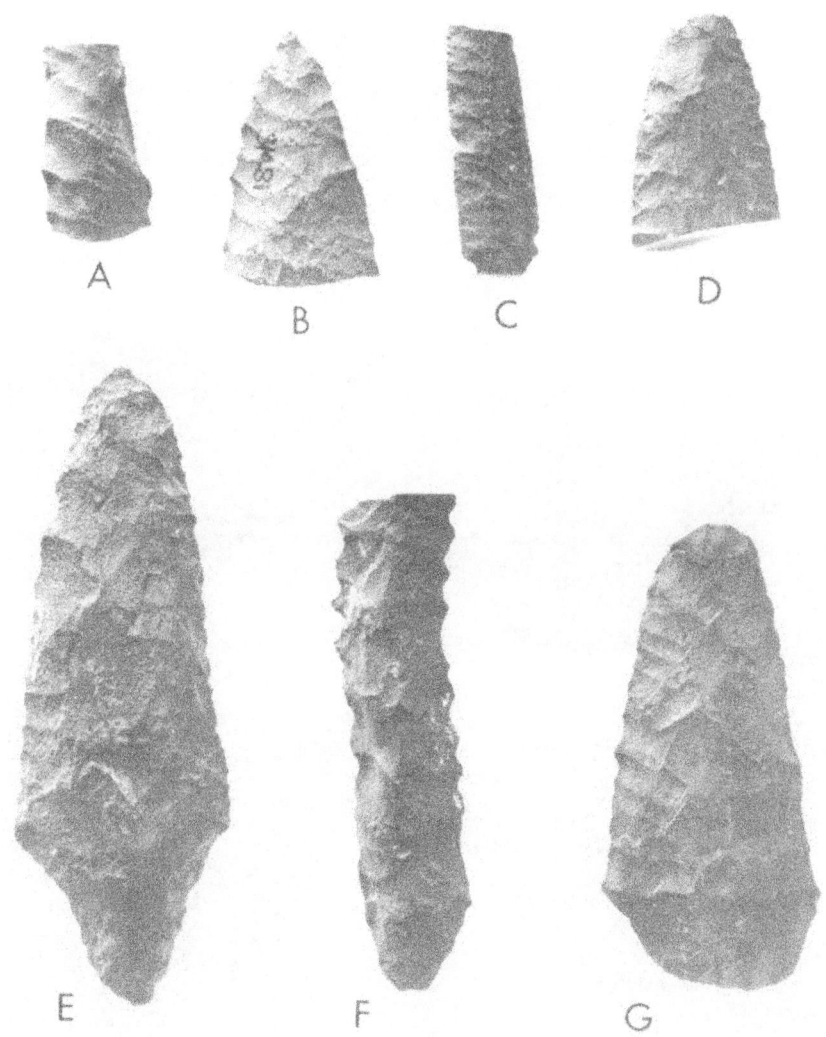

Projectile points. Specimen E is 8.8 cm long. A:32661, 2; B:31481, 4W, 2-3; C:31481, 4W, 2-3; D:32663, 3; E:32685, 4M, 1-2 (VIJ); F:32726, 4W, 3-4; G:32648, 1L (VIC). UMMA Neg. 11070.

PLATE XIV

Transverse side scrapers. Specimen A is 10.6 cm long. A:32704, 4M, 2-3; B:32666, 4M, 0-1 (VIIIC); C:32725, 4W, 3-4 (VIIIB); D:32687, 4M, 1-2; E:32666, 4M, 0-1. UMMA Neg. 11073.

PLATE XV

Blades; lateral and transverse side scrapers. Specimen A is 10.3 cm long. A:32720, 4M, 3-4; B:32666, 4M, 0-1; C:32687, 4M, 1-2 (VIIIA); D:32681, 4E, 1-2; E:32687, 4M, 1-2 (VIIIK); F:32671, 4W, 0-1. UMMA Neg. 11076.

PLATE XVI

Blades. Specimen D is 13.5 cm long. A:32687, 4M, 1-2; B:32799, 4, Fea. 1 (VIIE); C:32722, 4M, 3-4; D:32720, 4M, 3-4 (VIIF); E:31481, 4W, 2-3. UMMA Neg. 11077.

PLATE XVII

Blades. Specimen E is 16.3 cm long. A:32737, 4M, 4-5 (VIIIL); B:32737, 4M, 4-5 (VIIJ); C:32687, 4M, 1-2; D:32725, 4W, 3-4 (VIIC); E:31481, 4W, 2-3 (VIIB); F:32791, 4, Fea. 1. UMMA Neg. 11071.

PLATE XVIII

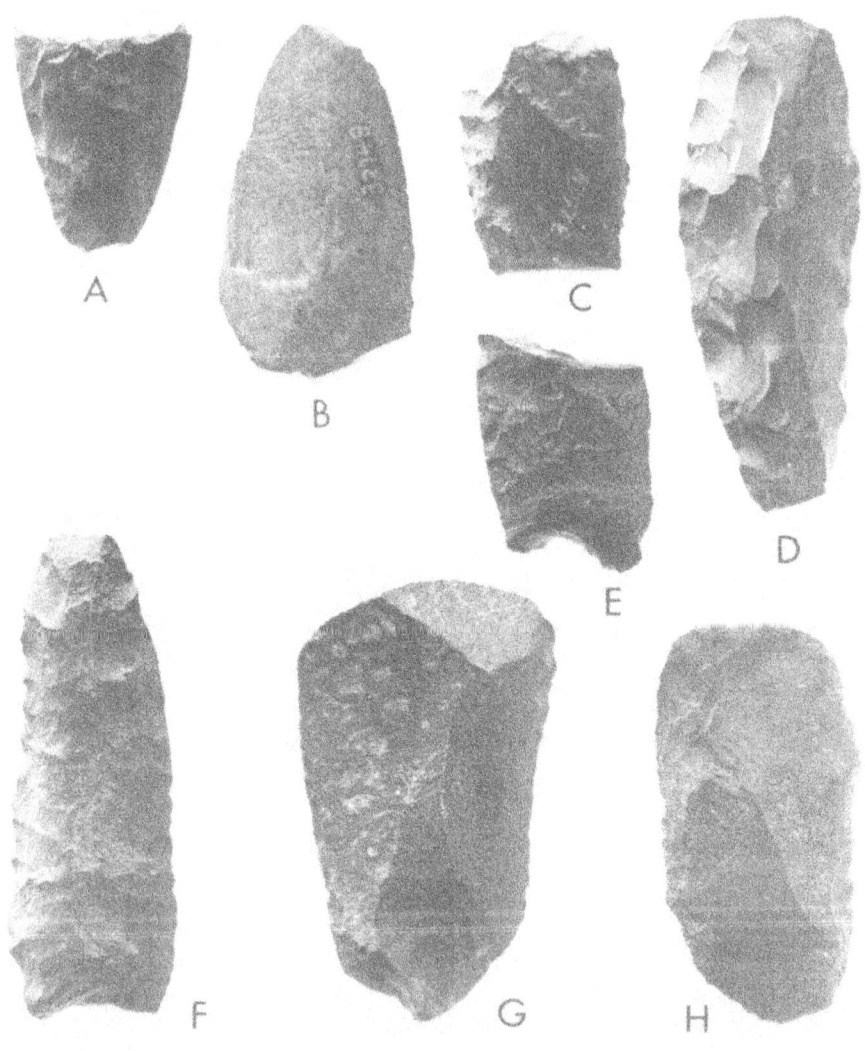

Scrapers; chisels and adzes (?); ground-stone knife or point. Specimen F is 8.3 cm long. A:32674, 4E, 0-1 (VIIIJ); B:32749, 4W, 4-5; C:32691, 4W, 1-2; D:32694, 4E, 2-3 (VIIH); E:31481, 4W, 2-3 (VIG); F:32671, 4W, 0-1; G:32694, 4E, 2-3; H:32681, 4E, 1-2. UMMA Neg. 11074.

PLATE XIX

Scrapers; gravers; and serrated flake. Specimen G is 6.9 cm long. A:32691, 4W, 1-2 (VIIIE); B:31481, 4W, 2-3 (VIIID); C:32666, 4M, 0-1 (VIIIH); D:32745, 4W, 4-5 (VIII-I), E:32687, 4M, 1-2 (VIIIG), F:32687, 4M, 1-2; G:32686, 4M, 1-2 (VIIIF). UMMA Neg. 11075.

PLATE XX

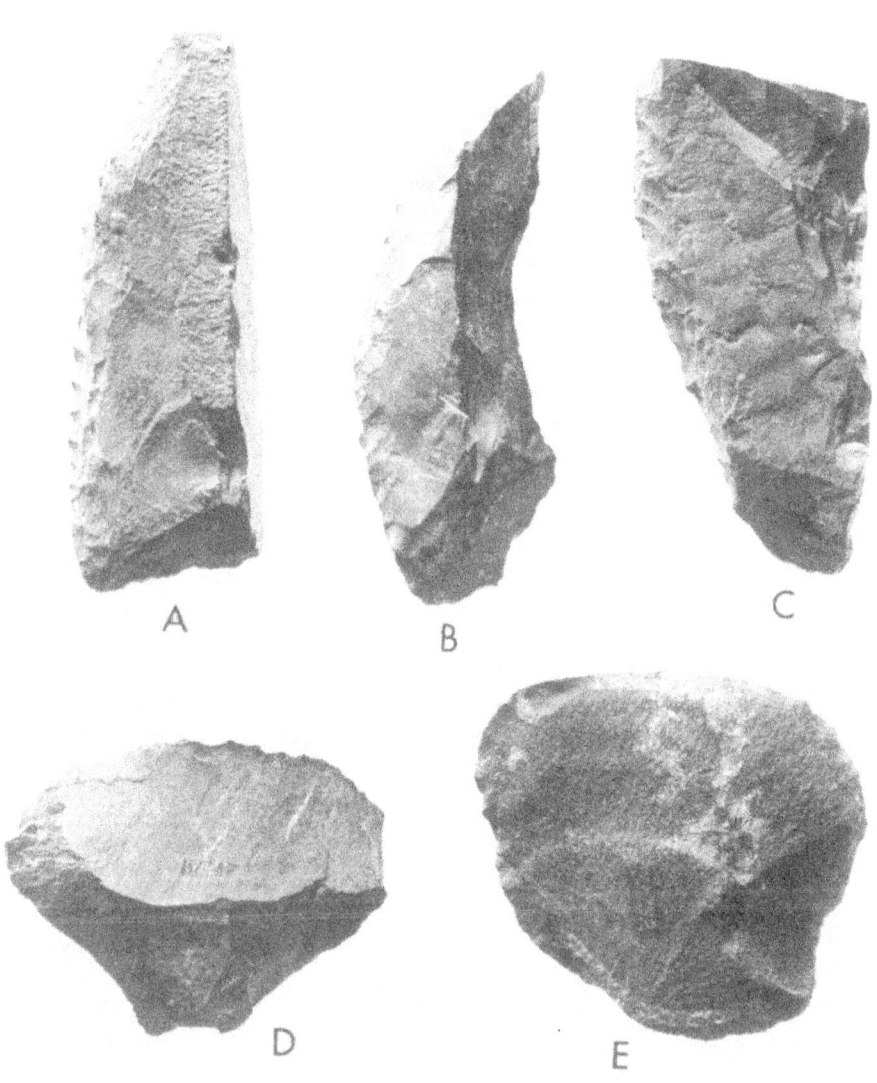

Transverse and lateral side scrapers. Specimen A is 11.9 cm long. A:32704, 4M, 2-3; B:32687, 4M, 1-2 (VIIIM); C:32704, 4M, 2-3; D:31481, 4W, 2-3; E:32752, 4M, 5-6. UMMA Neg. 11078.

PLATE XXI

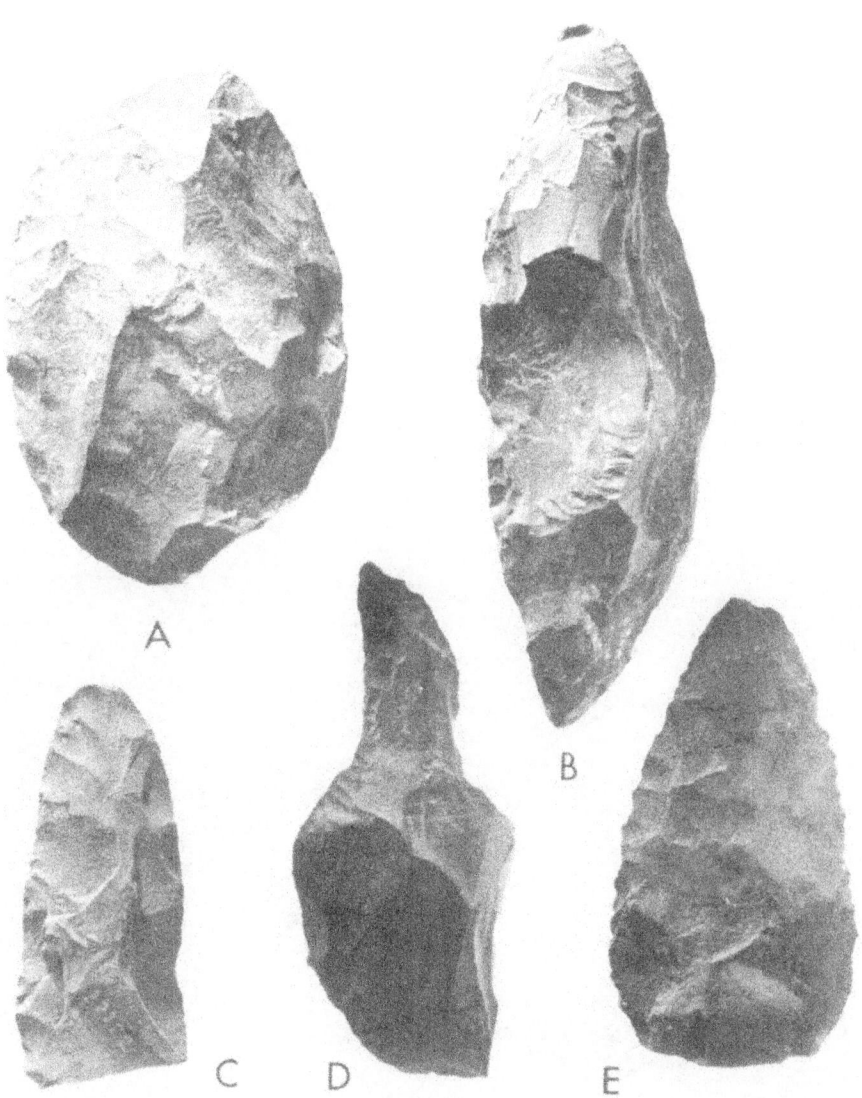

Blades and retouched flake knife or scraper. Specimen B is 15.2 cm long. A:32648, 1L (VIIG); B:32687, 4M, 1-2 (VIIA); C:32722, 4M, 3-4; D:32687, 4M, 1-2; E:31481, 4W,2-3. UMMA Neg. 11072.

PLATE XXII

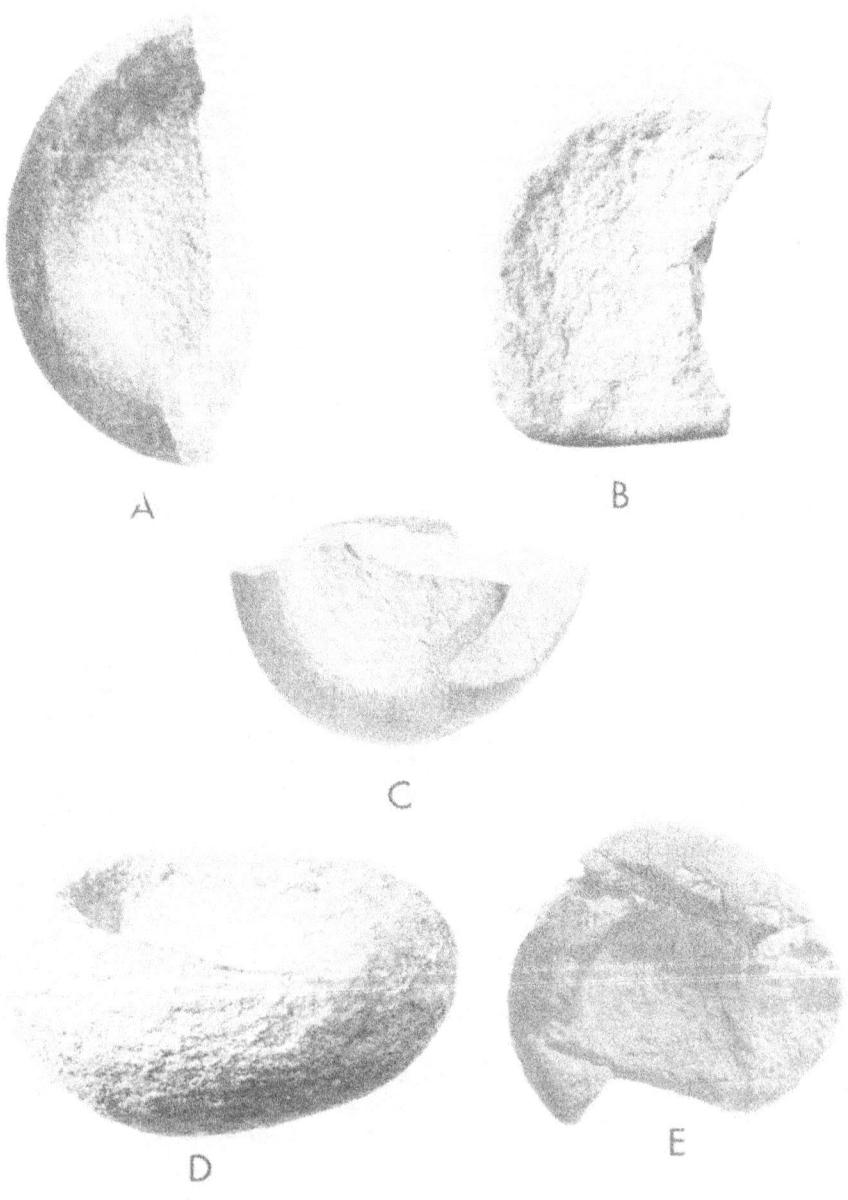

Stone lamps or vessels. Specimen A is 17.0 cm in diameter.
A:32699, 4W, 0-1; B:32744, 4W, 4-5; C:32793, 4, Fea. 3; D:32708, 4M,
2-3; E:32696, 4E, 2-3. UMMA Neg. 11082(C,E), 11083(B), 11084(A),
11085(D).

PLATE XXIII

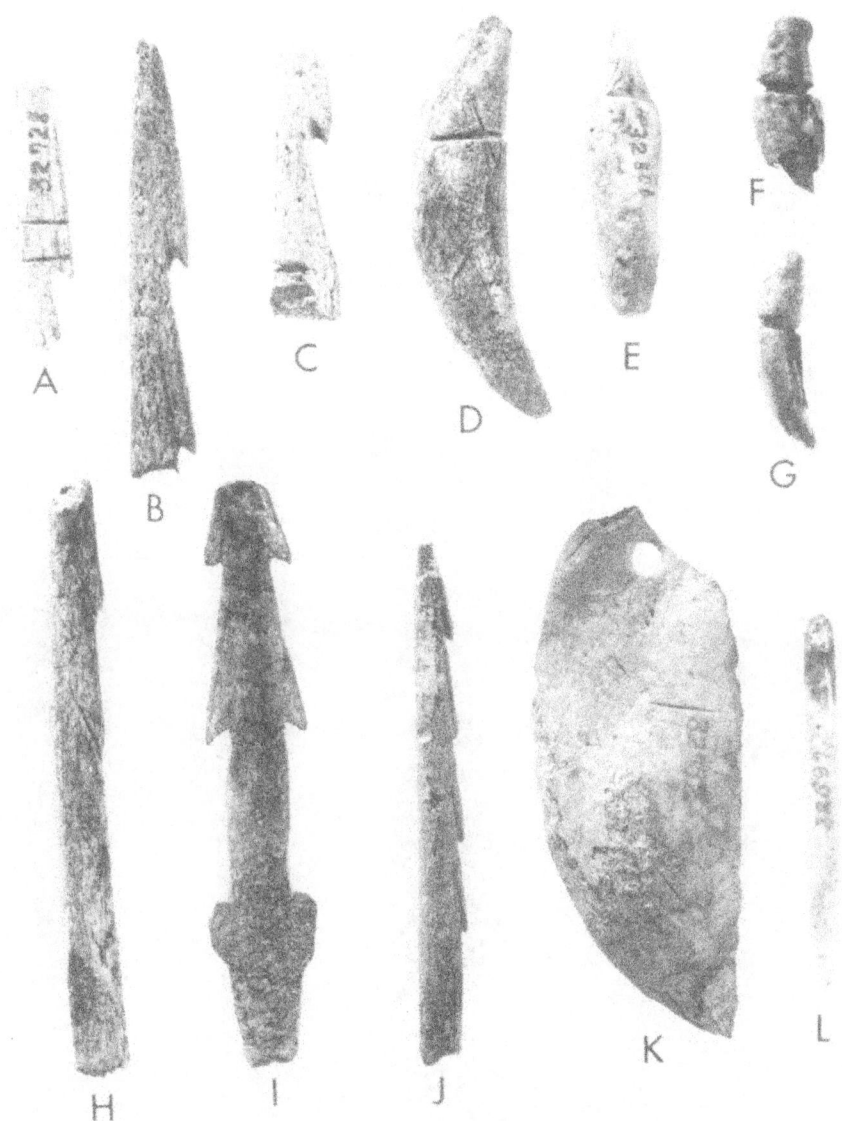

Barbed bone points and tooth ornaments. Specimen I is 9.5 cm long. A:32728, 4W, 3-4; B:32728, 4W, 3-4; C:32790, 4, Fea. 1; D:32796, 4, Fea. 1; E:32800, 4, Fea. 1; F:32801, 4, Fea. 1; G:32801, 4, Fea. 1; H:32728, 4W, 3-4; I:32775, 4M, below 7; J:32689, 4W, 1-2; K:32792, 4, Fea. 1; L:32697, 4E, 2-3. UMMA Neg. 11086.

PLATE XXIV

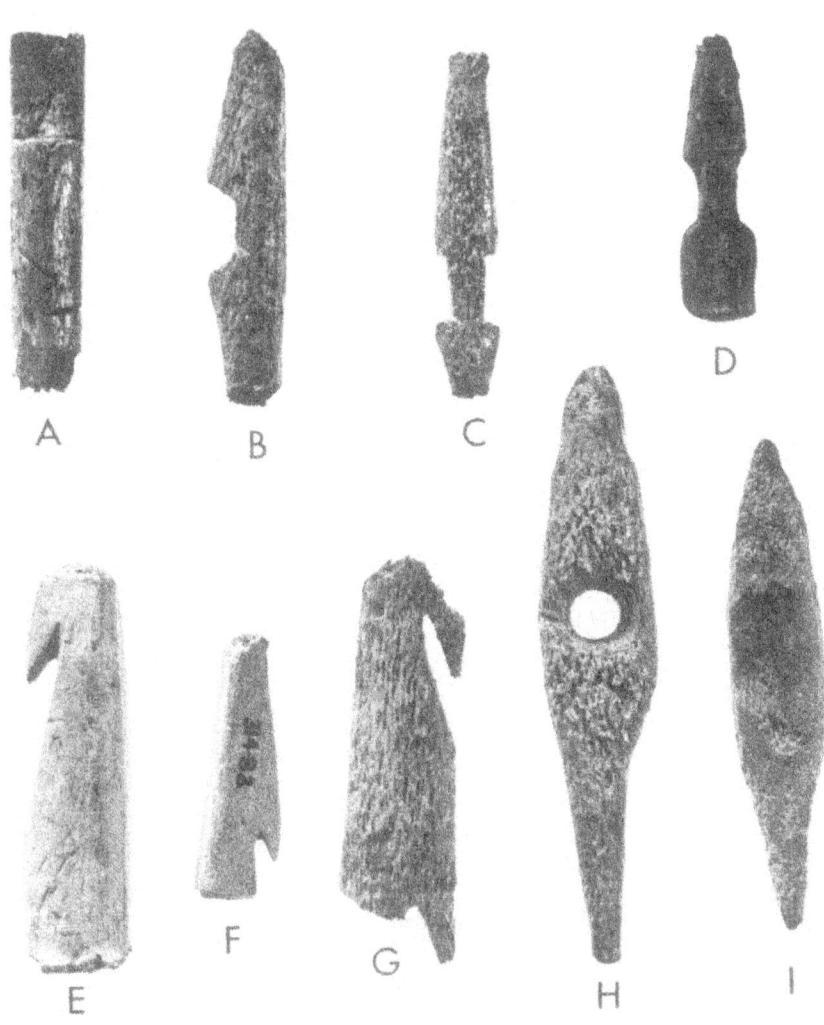

Bone and wood (D) projectile parts. Specimen H is 9.7 cm long.
A:32649, 1L; B:32784, 4W, 6-8; C:32763, 4W, 5-6; D:32804, 4, below
7.5; E:32755, 4M, 5-6; F:31482, 4W, 2-3; G:32748, 4W, 4-5; H:32729,
4W, 3-4; I:32776, 4M, below 7. UMMA Neg. 11090.

PLATE XXV

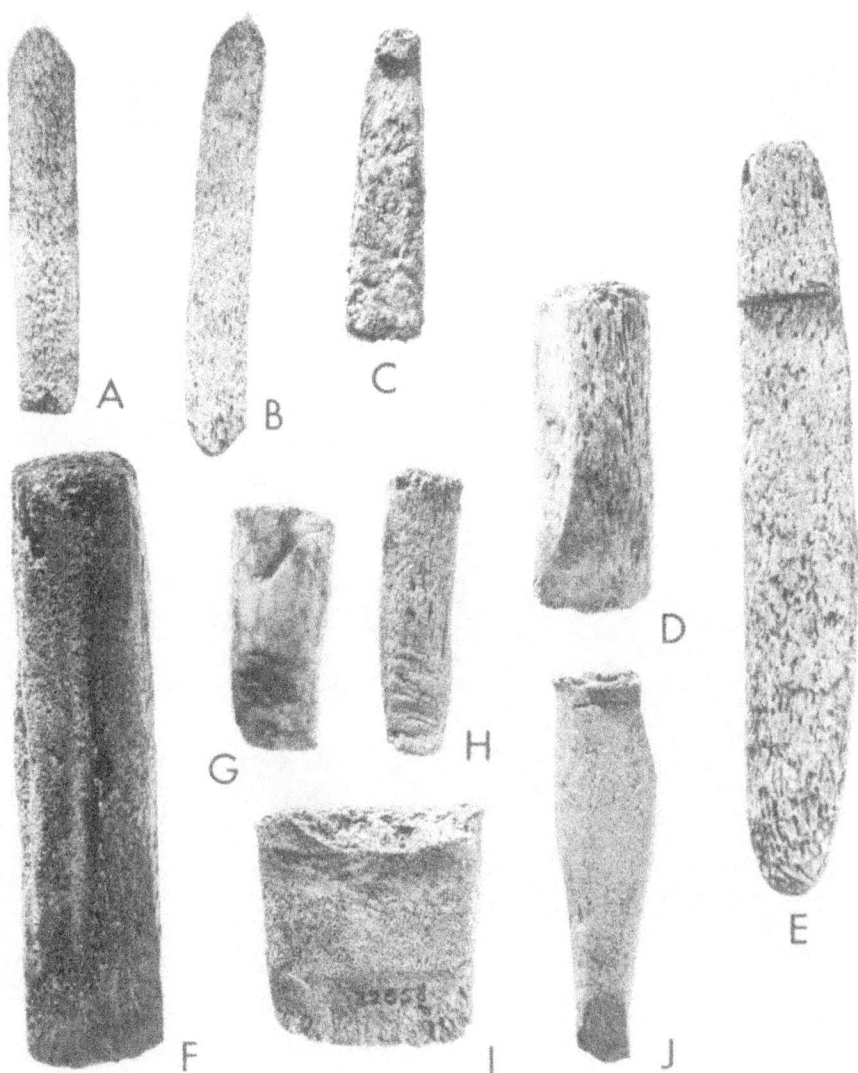

Bone flakers; bone and ivory wedges; bone handles (?). Specimen F is 12.9 cm long. A:32780, 4W, 7-8; B:32776, 4M, below 7; C:32649, 1L; D:32658, 2; E:32767, 4M, 6-7; F:32649, 1L; G:32739, 4M, 4-5; H:32761, 4W, 5-6; I:32658, 2; J:32746, 4W, 4-5. UMMA Neg. 11093.

PLATE XXVI

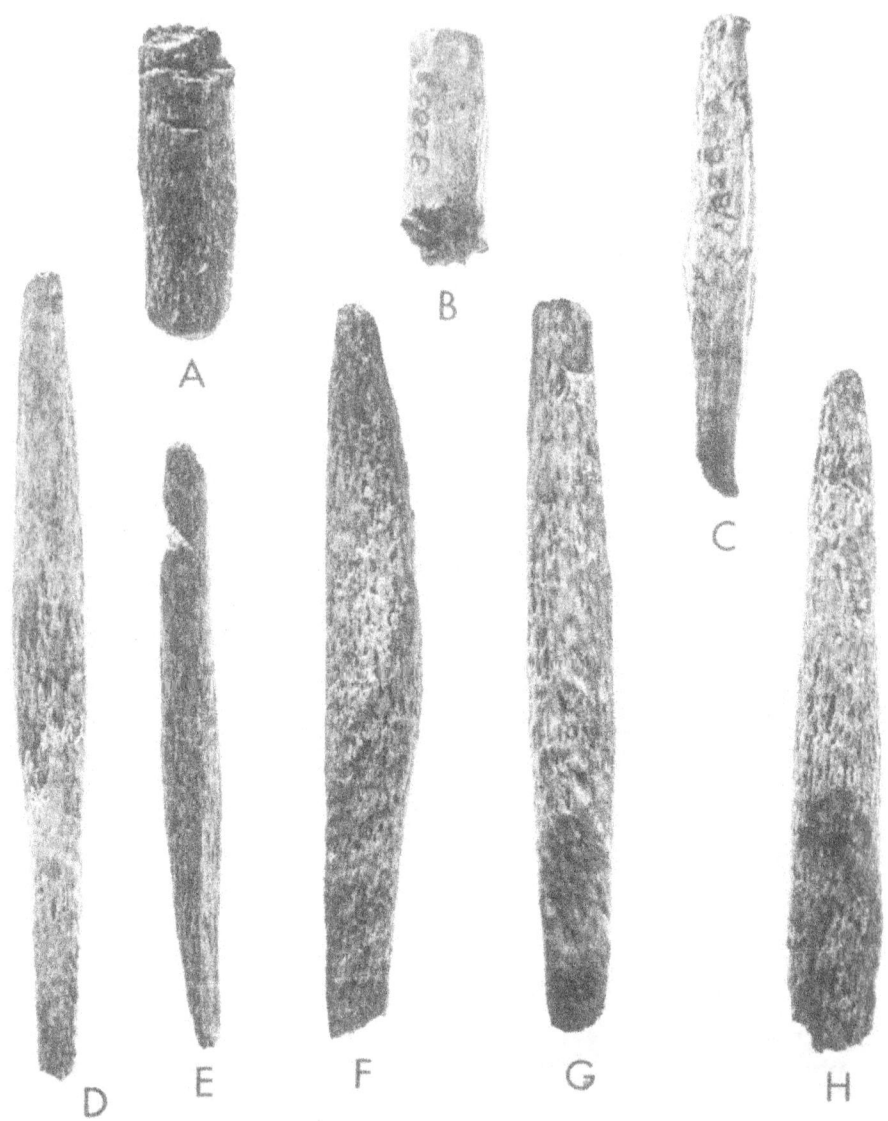

Bone cylinders (A and B) and prongs, or foreshafts, with beveled tangs. Specimen F is 11.1 cm long. A:32658, 2; B:32699, 4E, 2-3; C:32649, 1L; D:32740, 4M, 4-5; E:32678, 4M, 0-1; F:32731, 4W, 3-4; G:32692, 4W, 1-2; H:32787, 4. UMMA Neg. 11089.

PLATE XXVII

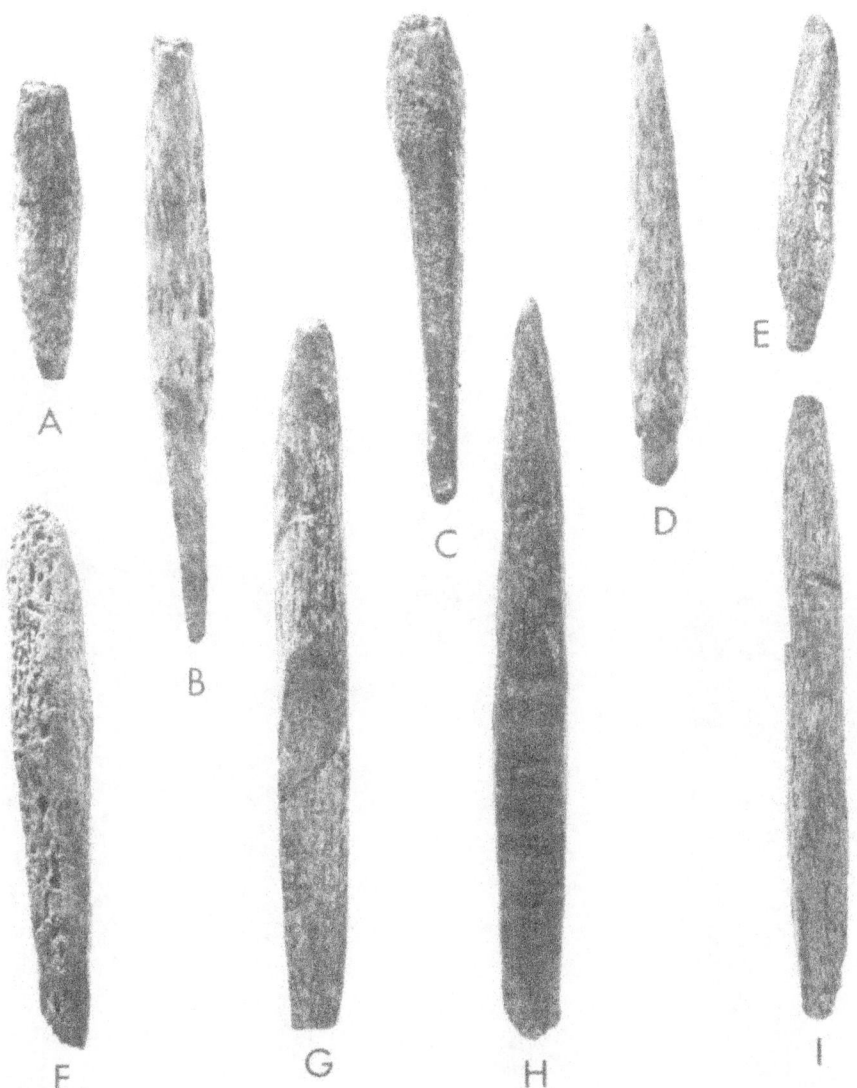

Bone prongs or foreshafts with beveled (F-I) or subconical tangs. Specimen G is 11.7 cm long. A:32776, 4M, below 7; B:32711, 4E, 3-4; C:32649, 1L; D:32742, 4M, 4-5; E:32692, 4W, 1-2; F:32798, 4, Fea. 1; G:32782, 4W, 7-8; H:32786, 4W, 6-8; I:32680, 4E, 1-2. UMMA Neg. 11087.

PLATE XXVIII

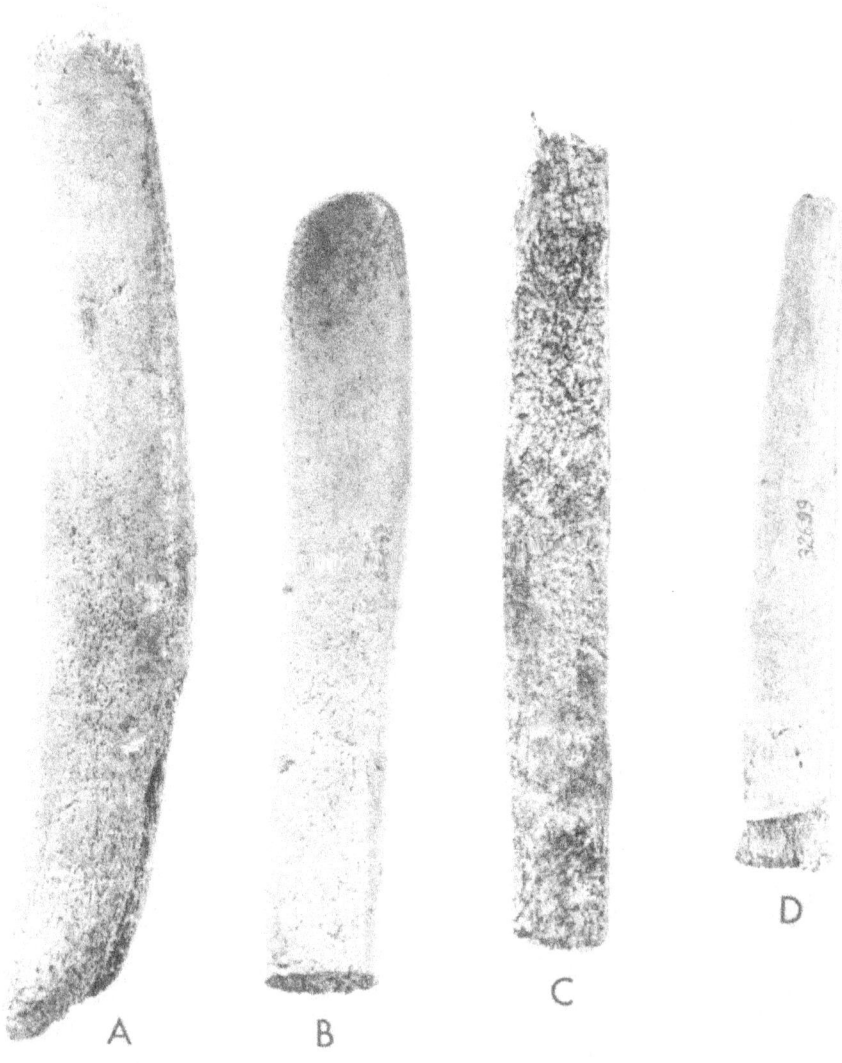

Worked ribs. Specimen A is 22.0 cm long. A:32761, 4W, 5-6; B:32678, 4M, 0-1; C:32649, 1L; D:32699, 4E, 2-3. UMMA Neg. 11088.

PLATE XXIX

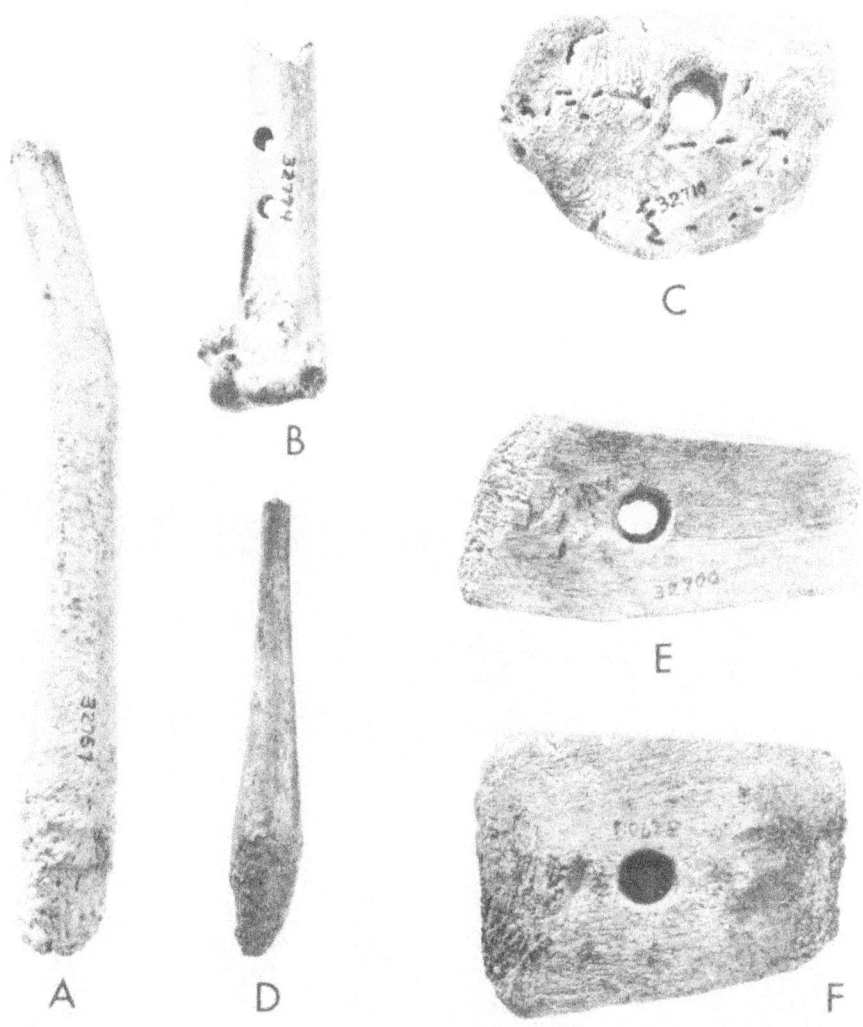

Baculum Flakers; perforated bird bone; bone (E and F) and fossil coral drill heads. Specimen A is 17.3 cm long. A:32767, 4M, 6-7; B:32774, 4M, below 7; C:32710, 4M, 2-3; D:32780, 4W, 7-8; E:32700, 4E, 2-3; F:32709, 4M, 2-3. UMMA Neg. 11091.

PLATE XXX

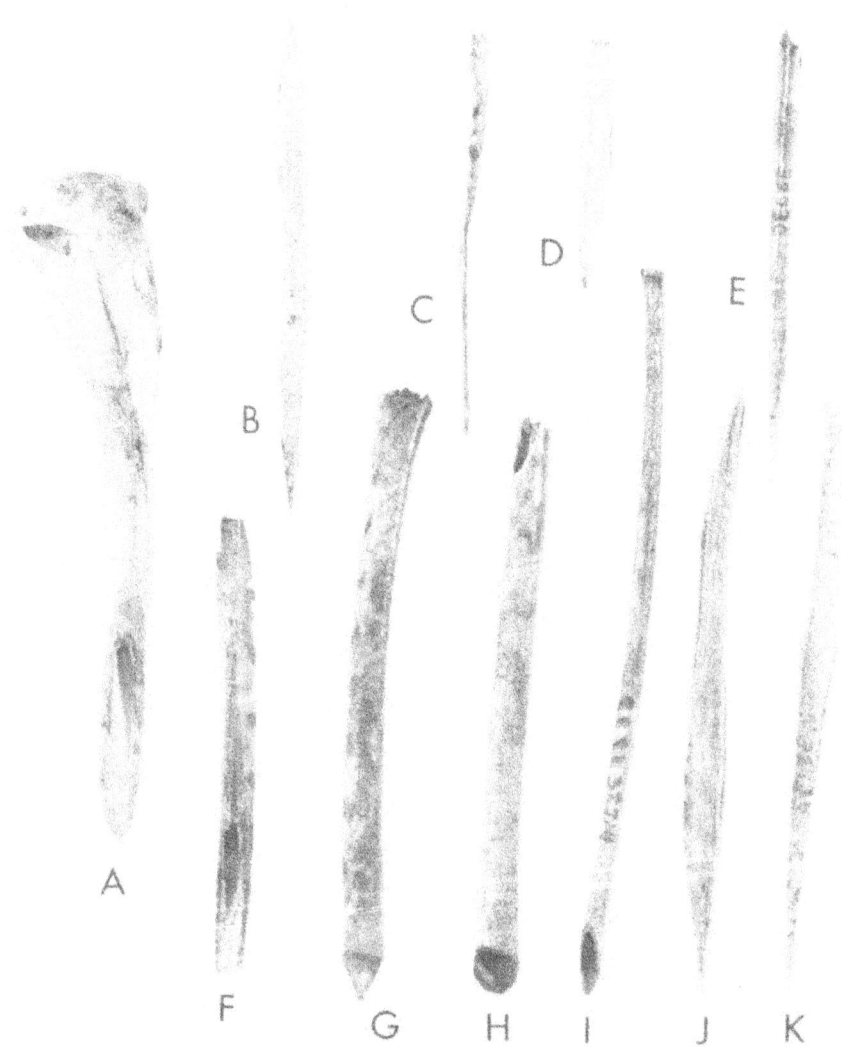

Bird-bone tools. Specimen A is 11.1 cm long. A:31482, 4W, 2-3; B:32692, 4W, 1-2; C:31482, 4W, 2-3; D:32798, 4, Fea. 1; E:32730, 4W, 3-4; F:32707, 4M, 2-3; G:32678, 4M, 0-1; H:32798, 4, Fea. 1; I:32714, 4E, 3-4; J:32692, 4W, 1-2; K:32733, 4W, 3-4. UMMA Neg. 11092.

PLATE XXXI

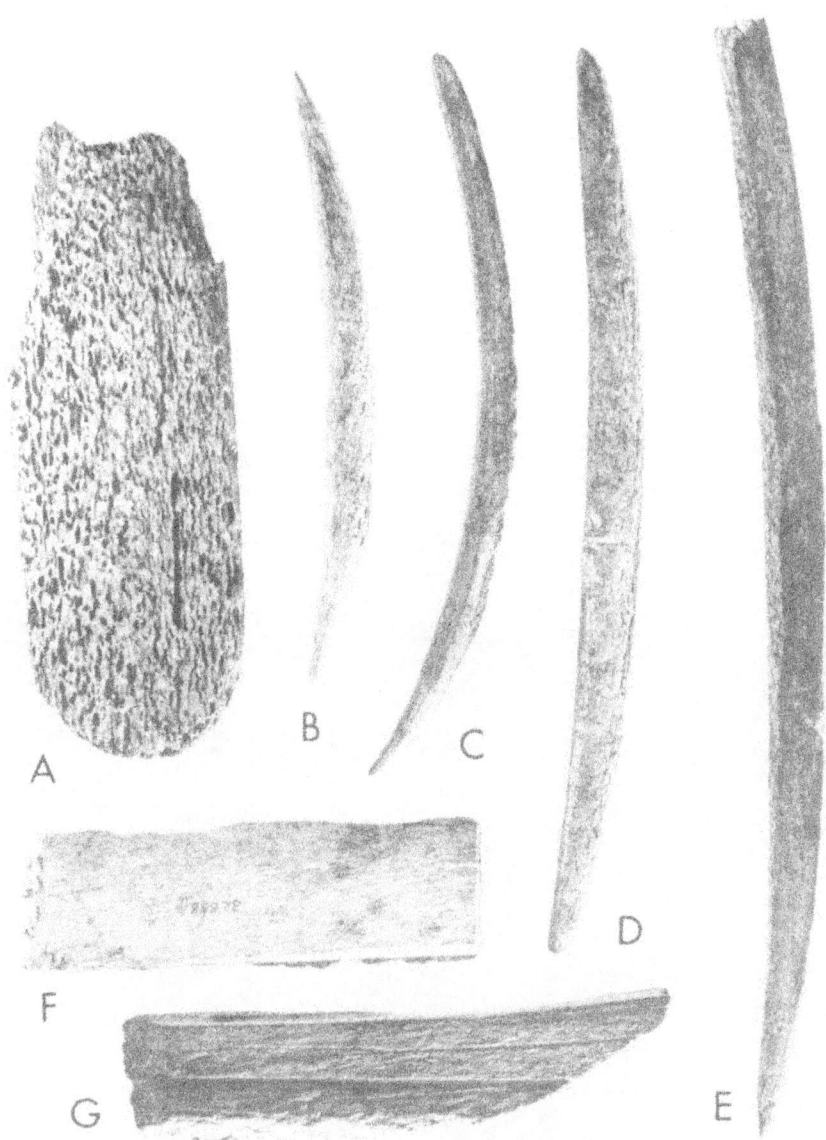

Worked whalebone (A, F, and G) and bone picks. Specimen E is 33.0 cm long. A:32680, 4E, 1-2; B:32658, 2; C:32781, 4W, 7-8; D:32776, 4M, below 7; E:32784, 4W, 6-8; F:32658, 2; G:32780, 4W, 7-8. UMMA Neg. 11094.

www.ingramcontent.com/pod-product-compliance
Lightning Source LLC
Jackson TN
JSHW070314120426
100741JS00007B/55